THE Quest FOR CHARACTER

Scripture quotations, unless otherwise marked, are taken from the New American Standard Bible, © The Lockman Foundation 1960, 1962, 1963, 1971, 1972, 1973, 1975, 1977, and are used by permission.

Scripture references marked NIV are from the Holy Bible: New International Version, copyright 1973, 1978, 1984 by the International Bible Society. Used by permission of Zondervan Bible Publishers.

Scripture references marked Phillips are taken from J.B. Phillips: The New Testament in Modern English, revised edition. © J.B. Phillips 1958, 1960, 1972.

Scripture quotations marked TLB are from The Living Bible, copyright 1971 by Tyndale House Publishers, Wheaton, Ill. Used by permission.

Cover design: Bruce DeRoos/Brenda Jose
Editor: Larry R. Libby
Author photo: G. Robert Nease

THE QUEST FOR CHARACTER
© by Charles R. Swindoll, Inc.
Published by Multnomah Press
Portland, Oregon 97266

Multnomah Press is a ministry of Multnomah School of the Bible, 8435 NE Glisan Street, Portland, Oregon 97220.

Printed in the United States of America

Library of Congress Cataloging-in-Publication Data

Swindoll, Charles R.
    Quest for character.

    1. Christian life.   2. Character.   I. Title.
BX6154.S92   1987   248.4   87-7825
ISBN 0-88070-200-1

87 88 89 90 91 92 93 94 95 — 9 8 7 6 5 4 3 2

THE Quest FOR CHARACTER

CHARLES R. SWINDOLL

This book is
affectionately dedicated
to my closest associates in ministry.

paul sailhamer

buck buchanan

doug haag

mel howell

howie stevenson

Their authenticity, consistency, integrity, and loyalty
have been of inestimable value to me
throughout our years together at
the First Evangelical Free Church of
Fullerton, California.
By their example I have become convinced
that the quest for character
is a goal worth pursuing.

contents

Part 1
GUARD YOUR HEART

contents

Part 2

GIVE YOUR HEART

james 1:2-4

When all kinds of trials and temptations crowd into your lives, my brothers, don't resent them as intruders, but welcome them as friends! Realize that they come to test your faith and to produce in you the quality of endurance. But let the process go on until that endurance is fully developed, and you will find you have become men of mature character, men of integrity with no weak spots (Phillips).

introduction

My first direct view of <u>Titanic</u> lasted less than two minutes, but the stark sight of her immense black hull towering above the ocean floor will remain forever ingrained in my memory. My lifelong dream was to find this great ship, and during the past thirteen years the quest for her had dominated my life. Now, finally, the quest was over.[1]

So wrote Robert Ballard after discovering the ghostly hulk of *H.M.S. Titanic* in her lonely berth more than two miles deep in the North Atlantic. For nearly three-quarters of a century, the grand old lady was celebrated in legend. Her skirt festooned by decades of decay and sediment. Her necklace tarnished and twisted. Though still impressive in her dimensions, her touch of elegance is gone. She is no longer the graceful maiden who slipped away on her first date in early April 1912. A mere five days into her romantic voyage, she was kidnapped and shortly thereafter killed by a cold, heartless iceberg lying in wait for her 350 miles southeast of Newfoundland.

The rest is familiar albeit tragic history. Alone and silent she has wept great tears of rust, not only for herself but even more so for those 1,522 souls who were taken with her.

Not until a strobe light penetrated her eerie, muddy grave on September 1, 1985, did anyone know for sure her whereabouts. On that eventful day the man who loved her too much to forget her, whose last thirteen years had been "dominated" by his "quest for her," caught his first glimpse. How fascinated was he by the maiden's appearance? Enough to take 53,500 photos of her. Enough to study every possible foot of her gigantic frame . . . 882 1/2 feet long, 92 1/2 feet wide, 46,328 tons heavy. Enough to respect her privacy and leave her as he found her, undisturbed and unexploited, once his checklist was complete. As Ballard wrote following his final visit, ". . . the quest for *Titanic* is over. May she now rest in peace."[2] Mission accomplished.

On several occasions the explorer used the same word to describe his lifelong dream: "quest." A quest is a pursuit, a search. Webster adds a colorful dimension to the definition ". . . a chivalrous enterprise in medieval romance usually involving an adventurous journey." That would probably make Robert Ballard smile. In a strange sort of way his adventurous journey was indeed a romance with a lady many years his senior.

What is *your* quest? Do you have a "lifelong dream"? Anything "dominating your life" enough to hold your attention for thirteen or more years? Some "adventurous journey" you'd love to participate in . . . some discovery you long to make . . . some enterprise you secretly imagine? Without a quest, life is quickly reduced to bleak black and wimpy white, a diet too bland to get anybody out of bed in the morning. A quest fuels our fire. It refuses to let us drift downstream gathering debris. It keeps our mind in gear, makes us press on. All of us are surrounded by and benefit from the results of someone else's quest. Let me name a few.

- Above my head is a bright electric light. *Thanks, Edison.*
- On my nose are eyeglasses that enable me to focus. *Thanks, Franklin.*
- In my driveway is a car ready to take me wherever I choose to steer it. *Thanks, Ford.*
- Across my shelves are books full of interesting and carefully researched pages. *Thanks, authors.*
- Flashing through my mind are ideas, memories, stimulating thoughts, and creative skills. *Thanks, teachers.*
- Deep inside me are personality traits, strong convictions, a sense of right and wrong, a love for God, an ethical compass, a lifelong commitment to my wife and family. *Thanks, parents.*
- Tucked away in the folds of my life are discipline and determination, a refusal to quit when the going gets rough, a love for our country's freedom, a respect for authority. *Thanks, Marines.*
- Coming into my ears through the day are sounds of beautiful music, each piece representing a different mix of melody and rhythm . . . lyrics that linger. *Thanks, composers.*
- At home are peaceful and magnetic surroundings, eye-pleasing design, colorful wallpaper, tasteful and comfortable furnishings, hugs of affirmation, a shelter in a time of storm. *Thanks, Cynthia.*

My list could continue another page. So could yours. Because some cared enough to dream, to pursue, to follow through and complete their quest, our lives are more comfortable, more stable. If nothing else, that is enough to spur me on.

How about you? Are you dreaming about writing an article or a book? Write it! Are you wondering if all that work with the kids is worth it? It's worth it. Keep pursuing! Want to go back to school and finish that degree? Go back and do it . . . pay the price, even if it takes years! In the middle of redecorating and getting tired of the mess? Stay at it! Trying to master a skill that takes time, patience, and energy (not to mention money)? Press on! Can't get that tune out of your head . . . got some songs that need to get on paper? See it through. Work at it! Thinking about going into business for yourself? Why not? It's hard to find real satisfaction halfway up someone else's corporate ladder.

God is forever on a quest. Ever thought about that? His pursuit is a subject woven through the fabric of the New Testament. The pattern He follows is set forth in Romans 8:29, where He promises to conform us to His Son's image. Another promise is stated in Philippians 1:6, where we're told He began His work in us and He isn't about to stop. Elsewhere He even calls us His "workmanship" (Ephesians 2:10). He is hammering, filing, chiseling, and shaping us! Peter's second letter goes so far as to *list* some of the things included in this quest—diligence, faith, moral excellence, knowledge, self-control, perseverance, godliness, kindness, and love (2 Peter 1:5-7). In a word . . . character.

Character qualities in His children—that's God's relentless quest. His strobe light will continue to penetrate our darkness. He won't quit His quest until He completes His checklist. And when will that be? When we rest in peace . . . and not one day sooner. Only then will His mission be accomplished in us. We have Him to thank for not giving up as we go through the process of developing character. *Thanks, Lord.*

This is a book about that. It is not intended to be an exhaustive list of all the qualities we need to address, not by a long shot. But it does include those that deserve our immediate attention. You see, God doesn't work in a vacuum. He could (and sometimes does), but when it comes to character traits, He gets us into the action. His quest becomes our quest. Concerns on His heart become concerns on our heart. I use the word "heart" because that's the term Scripture uses to describe the place where qualities worth having in our lives are first formed. Perhaps we could call the heart the womb of character.

Sometimes we are to guard our heart . . . protect it from invasion and keep things safe and secure. Sometimes we should give our heart . . . let certain qualities out and release them to others. Since both are true, I have divided the book according to that dual emphasis. The first twenty readings invite you to *guard your heart*, lest things that have no business being inside break and enter. The last twenty readings challenge you to *give your heart*, releasing traits that need to be put to use for the good of others and to the glory of God.

Hats off to several people who played vital roles in this volume. At Multnomah Press, Larry Libby, my long-time friend and editor, along with those inimitable, creative skills of Brenda Jose, provided invaluable assistance and encouragement. I am indebted to both for their competence, cooperation, and confidence. At the office, Helen Peters, my faithful, consistent secretary, who has labored with me through all my published works, deserves another round of applause. As I have traveled about, jotted down my thoughts, gathered them into a pile, then placed them before her in every imaginable condition, she has graciously accepted the challenge and diligently typed the manuscript. At home, Cynthia, Colleen, and Chuck have neither failed to understand my love for writing nor made me feel guilty when the deadline forced me to say no to them and yes to this. Rather, they have decreased their demands and lowered their expectations. They have even smiled understandingly at my preoccupation when my body was there but my head was here. Three cheers for those three C's!

Now, finally, to borrow from Robert Ballard, my quest is over. Well, at least this one you hold in your hands. That other one—the much larger one I write about all the way through my book—will never be over, not until I rest in peace. I will be guarding and giving my heart for the rest of my life. God will never stop hammering those things in me that need to be nailed down or filing my sharp edges or shaping my will or chipping and chiseling away on my attitude. Unlike the man who completed his quest when he located the Titanic, I will be on the quest for character throughout my days. And so will you.

My great desire is that these pages will give us longer patience during the process, and stronger endurance until the end. When this quest is finally over, count on it, we'll be in His glorious presence, conformed to the image of His Son.

Chuck Swindoll
Fullerton, California

THE HIGHEST REWARD
FOR A MAN'S TOIL
IS NOT
WHAT HE GETS FOR IT,
BUT RATHER
WHAT HE BECOMES BY IT.
—*AMERICAN WAY*

Part 1

=== GUARD YOUR HEART ===

Life is a jungle.

Who hasn't been up to his armpits in the quicksand of deadlines and demands? Who hasn't done battle with alligatorlike irritations in the slimy swamp of over-commitment, underachievement, and burnout? On top of all that are those surprise attacks from criticism that lunge at us like a hungry lion and tear into us like a panther's claw. Only the fit survive. And among the ones who do, those who sense danger and know the techniques of self-defense come through in the best condition.

Jay Rathman is such a man. While hunting deer in the Tehema Wildlife Area near Red Bluff in northern California, he climbed to a ledge on the slope of a rocky gorge. As he raised his head to look over the ledge above, he sensed movement to the right of his face. A coiled rattler struck with lightning speed, just missing Rathman's right ear.

The four-foot snake's fangs got snagged in the neck of Rathman's wool turtleneck sweater, and the force of the strike caused it to land on his left shoulder. It then coiled around his neck.

He grabbed it behind the head with his left hand and could feel the warm venom running down the skin of his neck, the rattles making a furious racket.

He fell backward and slid headfirst down the steep slope through brush and lava rocks, his rifle and binoculars bouncing beside him.

"As luck would have it," he said in describing the incident to a Department of Fish and Game official, "I ended up wedged between some rocks with my feet caught uphill from my head. I could barely move."

He got his right hand on his rifle and used it to disengage the fangs from his sweater, but the snake had enough leverage to strike again.

"He made about eight attempts and managed to hit me with his nose just below my eye about four times. I kept my face turned so he couldn't get a good angle with his fangs, but it was very close. This chap and I were eyeball to eyeball and I found out that snakes don't blink. He had fangs like darning needles. . . . I had to choke him to death. It was the only way out. I was afraid that with all the blood rushing to my head I might pass out."

When he tried to toss the dead snake aside, he couldn't let go—"I had to pry my fingers from its neck."

Rathman, 45, who works for the Defense Department in San Jose, estimates his encounter with the snake lasted 20 minutes.

Warden Dave Smith says of meeting Rathman: "He walked toward me holding this string of rattles and said with a sort of grin on his face, 'I'd like to register a complaint about your wildlife here.'"[3]

When I first read that hair-raising account, I thought about how closely Rathman's struggle resembles life on a daily basis. At the most unsuspecting moment we are pounced upon. With treacherous strength these snakelike assaults have a way of knocking us off balance as they wrap themselves around us. Exposed and vulnerable, we can easily succumb to the attacks. They are frequent and varied: physical pain, emotional trauma, relational stress, spiritual doubts, marital conflicts, carnal temptations, financial reversals, demonic assaults, occupational disappointments . . . whap whap, whap, *whap, WHAP*!

Relentlessly, we struggle for survival, knowing that any one of those strikes can hit the target and spread poison that can immobilize and paralyze, rendering us ineffective. And what exactly is that target? The heart. That's what the Bible calls it. Our inner person. Down deep, where hope is born, where decisions are made, where commitment is strengthened, where truth is stored, mainly where *character* (the stuff that gives us depth and makes us wise) is formed.

No wonder the wise man of old warns:

Listen, my son, and be wise,
and keep your heart on the right path (Proverbs 23:19, NIV).

The quest for character requires that certain things be kept *in* the heart as well as kept *from* the heart. An unguarded heart spells disaster. A well-guarded heart means survival. If you hope to survive the jungle, overcoming each treacherous attack, you'll have to guard your heart.

The pages that follow will encourage you to do that.

targets of temptation

Fortune. Fame. Power. Pleasure. When it comes to temptation, these are the biggies.

Not that there are no other snags and pitfalls; there are. But these four represent the weakest links in our chain of resistance . . . the most obvious chinks in our armor. If the enemy of our souls wants to launch one of his "flaming missiles" toward an area that will have the greatest impact, he's got a choice of four major targets.

FORTUNE. Money, money, money. Stuff that has a price tag. Material goods. Tangible things. And behind all that? The desire to own, to possess, to amass wealth, to get rich; let's face it, to *look* rich. This is that deep-seated craving to impress others as well as to scratch the age-old itch for more. Always more. Enough is never enough. Contentment is out of the question.

All this seems so clear on paper. Color it green and call it greed, plain and simple . . . easy to analyze at this objective moment; it's obvious. But somehow when we slip into the mainstream and begin to swim, there's that current (so subtle to begin with) that surrounds us and tugs at us. Before long we are swept up in it, plunging toward the rapids, almost out of control. To break free and chart an alternate course (never subtle, never easy!) requires nothing less than the power of Almighty God. Nobody ever withstood greed without a fight that was both relentless and fierce. The god Fortune dies a slow, painful death.

FAME. This is the push to be popular. To be "one of the gang." To be liked. Actually, it is more than that. It's the hunger to be known, to make a name for oneself. It includes jockeying for the top spot, shaking the right hands, patting the right backs, being in the right spots . . . adroitly manipulating and maneuvering. All the while there is the unspoken preoccupation with a hidden egocentric agenda: Get your name up there in the lights. The insecurity this reveals is somewhere between pathetic and nauseating.

Don't misunderstand. For some, fame comes by surprise. It's nothing more than a by-product of a job well done, free from strategy. With no interest in being known, some are thrust onto center stage quite apart from their own desire. No problem, just so they keep examining their motives and maintaining their equilibrium. Fame can be heady stuff. Heights easily make heads swim. As one wag put it, "Fame, like flame, is harmless until you start inhaling it."[4] People who handle it graciously don't let themselves forget how undeserving they are. Frequently, their roots can be traced to the most humble of origins. Like the famous black contralto, Marian Anderson, who claimed that the greatest moment of her life occurred the day she went home and told her mama she wouldn't have to take in washing anymore.

POWER. Those seeking power want to control, to rule over others. They want to take charge and get their way. They manipulate and manuever to be in a position of authority so they can hold others in check or force them to get in line. Though some accomplish this as masters of deceit, hiding the real truth behind smiling masks and pious words, their domineering style becomes evident when those who are supposed to follow don't, but rather exert some healthy and creative independence. "Anathema!" cries the ruler. "Zap!" goes the whip. Power people have little tolerance for folks who think on their own and speak their mind.

For some strange reason the religious ranks are swollen with those who have yielded to this particular temptation. Give certain people enough authority to lead, a Bible to quote, and a need to succeed, and before long you'd think Caesar had been reincarnated. It's no surprise that Peter, when addressing those who shepherd the flock of God, warned against "lording it over those allotted to your charge" (1 Peter 5:3). Power-mad leaders leave more battered sheep than we would ever believe. And the special tragedy of that is that battered sheep don't reproduce, and they seldom fully recover.

PLEASURE. "If it feels good . . ." Aw, you can finish the saying. Perhaps our most vulnerable point of temptation, pleasure represents the desire to be sensually satisfied no matter the cost. It may be as harmless as an amusement or as sordid as an illicit sexual encounter. The act is not my point, the attitude is. "I want what I want when I want it. I am going to be happy, I need to be fulfilled, my desires will be gratified . . . regardless!"

No, no, we never come out and say it that boldly. But it is with that level of intensity that sensual pleasure is pursued. And in doing so we rationalize around Scripture, we lower our standard of morality, we ignore the promptings of our conscience, thus convincing ourselves that it's not merely okay, it is a *necessity!* And if somehow visions of a holy God interrupt our fun on the playground, we have ways of ignoring Him, too. Paul portrays such people as "fools":

> *For even though they knew God, they did not honor Him as God . . . but they became futile in their speculations, and their foolish heart was darkened. Professing to be wise, they became fools* (Romans 1:21-22).

Fortune. Fame. Power. Pleasure. When it comes to temptation, these are the biggies. By resisting each, out in the open, we cultivate character down inside. So keep your eyes open and your shield handy. The battle is on right now. You can't trust Satan's cease-fires.

Above all be sure you take faith as your shield, for it can quench every burning missile the enemy hurls at you (Ephesians 6:16, Phillips).

The apostle John writes strong words in 1 John 5:19: "The whole world lies in the power of the evil one." And then he warns, "Little children, guard yourselves from idols." Idols like fortune, fame, power, and pleasure. That's one of the reasons quiet moments with the Lord are so valuable. To clear our focus. To correct our vision. To kindle our praise. To redirect our priorities. To shift our attention from this planet to eternal things.

Read 1 John 5.

true success

It doesn't say enough, but what it does say is good. I'm referring to Ralph Waldo Emerson's reflections on success.

> How do you measure success?
> To laugh often and much;
> To win the respect of intelligent people
>   and the affection of children;
> To earn the appreciation of honest critics
>   and endure the betrayal of false friends;
> To appreciate beauty;
> To find the best in others;
> To leave the world a bit better
>   whether by a healthy child,
>   a redeemed social condition,
>   or a job well done;
> To know even one other life has breathed
>   because you lived—
>   this is to have succeeded.[5]

I'm impressed. I appreciate what *isn't* mentioned as much as what is. Emerson doesn't once refer to money, status, rank, or fame. He says nothing about power over others, either. Or possessions. Or a super-intimidating self-image. Or emphasis on size, numbers, statistics, and other visible nonessentials in light of eternity.

Read his words again. Maybe you missed something the first time around. Pay closer attention to the verbs this time: "to laugh . . . to win . . . to earn . . . endure . . . to appreciate . . . to find . . . to leave . . . to know. . . ." And all the way through, the major emphasis is outside of ourselves, isn't it? I find that the most refreshing part of all. It's also rare among success-oriented literature.

As I wade through the success propaganda written today, again and again the focus of attention is on one's outer self— how smart I can appear, what a good impression I can make, how much I can own or how totally I can control or how fast I can be promoted or . . . or . . . or. Nothing I read—and I mean *nothing*— places emphasis on the heart, the inner being, the seed plot of our thoughts, motives, decisions. Nothing, that is, except Scripture.

Interestingly, the Bible says little about success, but a lot about heart, the place where true success originates. Small wonder Solomon challenges his readers:

> *Above all else, guard your heart,*
> *for it is the wellspring of life* (Proverbs 4:23, NIV).

That's right—*guard* it. Put a sentinel on duty. Watch it carefully. Protect it. Pay attention to it. Keep it clean. Clear away the debris. It's there, remember, that bad stuff can easily hide out, like:

. . . evil thoughts, sexual immorality, theft, murder, adultery, greed, malice, deceit, lewdness, envy, slander, arrogance and folly (Mark 7:21-22, NIV).

You know, all the things that finally emerge once the heady, sweet smell of success intoxicates us, causing "the wellspring of life" to splash all around. How important is the heart! It is there that character is formed. It alone holds the secrets of true success. Its treasures are priceless—but they can be stolen.

Are you guarding it? Honestly now, are you? Sin's ugly and poisonous roots find nourishment deep within our hearts. Though we look successful, sound successful, talk about success, and even dress for success, all the while our hearts may be on a drift. It is possible to be privately eroding from the very things our lips are publicly extolling. It's called pretending. A harsher term is hypocrisy . . . and successful people can be awfully good at that.

I have the late Joseph Bayly to thank for the following:

Jesus warned His disciples, we must beware of hypocrisy—pretending to be something we aren't, acting with a mask covering our face. Hypocrisy is a terrible sign of trouble in our hearts—it waits only for the day of exposure. For as John Milton put it in *Paradise Lost,* "Neither men nor angels can discern hypocrisy, the only evil that walks invisible—except to God."[6]

Emerson's thoughts on success are profound, well worth being memorized. But this business of the heart needs to be added. Guarding it is essential, not optional. It isn't easy. It won't come naturally. It requires honesty. It calls for purity.

✳ Successes can easily become failures. All it takes is letting our guard down. ✳

To be like Christ. That is our goal, plain and simple. It sounds like a peaceful, relaxing, easy objective. But stop and think. He learned obedience by the things He suffered. So do we. He endured all kinds of temptations. So must we. To be like Christ is our goal. But it is neither easy nor quick nor natural. It's impossible in the flesh, slow in coming, and supernatural in scope. Only Christ can accomplish it within us.

Read Mark 7:1-23.

group numbing

Tell me, where were you the morning of March 16, 1968? I can't remember either. But there is a group of men who can't forget. Even though they'll never be together again, *that* morning will never be forgotten.

The guys had a tough assignment . . . one of those search-and-destroy missions, a combat element of *Task Force Barker*, assigned to move into a small group of hamlets known collectively as MyLai (Me-Lie) in the Quang Ngai province of South Vietnam. Hastily trained and thrown together, most were inexperienced in battle. For a whole month prior to MyLai, they had achieved no military success. Although unable to engage the Vietcong in actual combat, they had nevertheless sustained a number of demoralizing casualties from land mines and nasty booby traps. Add to this poor food, thick swarms of insects, oppressive heat, jungle humidity and rain, plus loss of sleep, and you've got the makings of madness. And confusion as to the identity of the enemy didn't help either. Vietnamese and Vietcong looked the same. Since so few wore uniforms, distinguishing combatants from noncombatants was more than difficult. Would you believe *impossible?*

Looking back across the years since 1968, with the calm objectivity time and history provide, it's not an exaggeration to say that the instructions given to both enlisted men and junior officers the night before the assault were at best incomplete and ambiguous. All troops were supposed to be familiar with the Geneva Convention, which makes it a crime to harm any non-combatant (or, for that matter, even a combatant) who has laid down his arms because of wounds or sickness. It's probable that some of the troops were also unfamiliar with the "Law of Land Warfare" from the *United States Army Field Manual*, which specifies that orders in violation of the Geneva Convention are illegal and not to be obeyed. Period.

When "Charlie" Company moved nervously into the MyLai region that morning, they discovered not a single combatant. Nobody was armed. No one fired on them. There were only unarmed women, children, and old men.

The things that then occurred are somewhat unclear. No one can reproduce the exact order of events, but neither can anyone deny the tragic results: Between five hundred and six hundred Vietnamese were killed in various ways. In some cases, troops stood at the door of a village hut and sprayed into it with automatic and semi-automatic rifle fire, killing everyone inside. Others were shot as they attempted to run away, some with babies in their arms. The most large-scale killings occurred in the particular hamlet of MyLai 4 where the first platoon of "Charlie" Company, under the command of a young lieutenant named William L. Calley, Jr., herded villagers into groups of twenty to forty or more, then finished them off with rifle fire, machine guns, and/or grenades.

The killing took a long time, like the whole morning. The number of soldiers involved can only be estimated. Perhaps as few as fifty actually pulled triggers and yanked grenade pins, but it is fairly accurate to assume that about two hundred directly witnessed the slaughter. We might suppose that within a week at least five hundred men in *Task Force Barker* knew that war crimes had been committed. Eventually, you may remember, charges were to be considered against twenty-five, of whom only six were brought to trial. Finally, only one was convicted, Lieutenant Calley . . . though, if we got specific about it, many were guilty. I remind you, failure to report a crime is itself a crime. In the year that followed, guess how many in *Task Force Barker* attempted to report the killings. Not one.

The fact that the American public learned about MyLai at all was due solely to a letter that Ron Ridenhour wrote to several congressmen three months after his return to civilian life at the end of March 1969 . . . over one year after the massacre.

So much for March 16, 1968. It happened. It's over. It's not my desire to set myself up as judge and jury, to point a finger of guilt at a few more of those soldiers trying to survive on the ragged edge. The men don't need further condemnation (frankly, I admire them for even *being* there, trying to do their duty), but we can all benefit from a brief evaluation.

To me, MyLai is a classic illustration of what one professional has called "psychic numbing," which often occurs within a group . . . sort of an emotional self-anesthesia. In situations in which our emotional feelings are overwhelmingly painful or unpleasant, the group aids in the capacity to anesthetize one another. It is greatly encouraged by being in the midst of others doing the same thing. Instead of crisp thinking, distinctly weighing the rightness and wrongness of an act, we find it possible—even easy—to pass the moral buck to some other part of the group. In this way, not only does the individual forsake his or her conscience, but the conscience of the group as a whole becomes so fragmented and diluted that it becomes almost non-existent. As Dr. Scott Peck describes so vividly in his book *People of the Lie*, "It is a simple sort of thing . . . the horrible becomes normal and we lose our sense of horror. We simply tune it out."[7]

That explains why peer pressure is so powerful, so potentially dangerous. It's a major motivation behind experimentation with drugs or sexual promiscuity or wholesale commitment to some cult or cooperation with an illegal financial scheme. The smirks or shouts of the majority have a way of intimidating integrity. And if it can happen to soldiers in Southeast Asia it can just as surely happen to folks like you and me.

So be on guard! When push comes to shove, think independently. Think biblically. Do everything possible to lead with your head rather than your feelings. If you fail to do this, you'll lose your ethical compass somewhere between longing to be liked and desiring to do what is right.

"Do not be misled," warns the apostle who often stood alone, "bad company corrupts good character" (1 Corinthians 15:33, NIV). Group numbing has the possibility of hovering almost indefinitely in a conscienceless and evil holding pattern.

You question that? Consider Jonestown. Or Watergate. Or the LSD experiments conducted by the CIA. Or the Holocaust. Or the Inquisition. Or the group that screamed, "Crucify Him."

Tell me, is some group numbing you?

In an impersonal, fast-moving world where we feel more like a number than a person, it is easy to believe that our vertical relationship is much the same. Nameless faces before a preoccupied God; busy people involved in meaningless, futile activity. Not so. God's Word assures us of an identity and promises us that our lives have order, reason, and purpose. Let us live today with that comforting confidence . . . God knows what He is about.

Read Joshua 23:1-16; 24:14-15.

a caged killer

It happened many years ago.

A research psychologist at the National Institute of Mental Health was convinced he could prove his theory from a cage full of mice. His name? Dr. John Calhoun. His theory? Overcrowded conditions take a terrible toll on humanity.

Dr. Calhoun built a nine-foot square cage for selected mice. He observed them closely as their population grew. He started with eight mice. The cage was designed to contain comfortably a population of 160. He allowed the mice to grow, however, to a population of 2,200.

They were not deprived of any of life's necessities except privacy—no time or space to be all alone. Food, water, and other resources were always clean and in abundance. A pleasant temperature was maintained. No disease was present. All mortality factors (except aging) were eliminated. The cage, except for its over-crowded condition, was ideal for the mice. The population reached its peak at 2,200 after about two-and-a-half years. Since there was no way for the mice to physically escape from their closed environment, Dr. Calhoun was especially interested in how they would handle themselves in that overcrowded cage.

Interestingly, as the population reached its peak, the colony of mice began to disintegrate. Strange stuff started happening. Dr. Calhoun made these observations:

- Adults formed natural groups of about a dozen individual mice.
- In each group each adult mouse performed a particular social role . . . but there were no roles in which to place the healthy young mice, which totally disrupted the whole society.
- The males who had protected their territory withdrew from leadership.
- The females became aggressive and forced out the young . . . even their own offspring.
- The young grew to be only self-indulgent. They ate, drank, slept, groomed themselves, but showed no normal aggression and, most noteworthy, failed to reproduce.

After five years, *every mouse had died*. This occurred despite the fact that right up to the end there was plenty of food, water, and an absence of disease. After the research psychologist reported on his experiment, a couple of significant questions arose.

Q: "What were the first activities to cease?"
A: "The most complex activities for mice: courtship and mating."
Q: "What results would such overcrowding have on humanity?"
A: "We would first of all cease to reproduce our ideas, and along with ideas, our goals and ideals. In other words, our values would be lost."[8]

I confess, I'm a bit haunted by that experiment.

I know, I know. We're not mice. And we're not caged. And we're not that overcrowded; though it seems we come pretty close here in southern California!

Nevertheless, the experiment conveys a few analogies worth thinking over. Look back at that list of observations and draw your own conclusions. Don't miss a couple of Calhoun's remarks—one, an observation; the other, an opinion.

The Observation: "The young . . . failed to reproduce."

The Opinion: ". . . our values would be lost."

Though we've promised ourselves and the Lord it would be different this year, many of us continue to wrestle with a stubborn, eight-armed octopus called "busy-ness." We continually find ourselves pushing too hard, going to fast, trying to do too much. Am I right? The "tyranny of the urgent" has wrapped its powerful tentacles around yet another year, hasn't it? Even though you know that the secret of knowing God requires "being still" (Psalm 46:10—the Hebrew says, *Cease striving—let go, relax!*), you've already started rationalizing your busy-ness. By doing so, you have put the quest for character on hold.

Do you realize the dangers of a life without privacy? Are you aware that a lack of time to be alone initiates spiritual disintegration? To borrow from

Gordon MacDonald, "ordering your private world" gets lost in the shuffle.

No big deal? No problem? Don't bet on it! Learn a singular lesson from caged mice. The same killer is on the loose . . . not a lack of food and water, not a lack of health and activity, but a lack of time alone with God, away from the crowd. Keep the overcrowded schedule up and your young will fail to reproduce the qualities worth living for . . . and you yourself will lose the values worth dying for.

Remember what happened many years ago. Not one creature survived those overcrowded conditions, yet their lesson speaks loud and clear to us this very moment.

These are the mice that roared.

TODAY'S
Quest

To be used of God. Is there anything more encouraging, more fulfilling? Perhaps not, but there is something more basic: to meet with God. To linger in His presence, to shut out the noise of the city and, in quietness, give Him the praise He deserves. Before we engage ourselves in His work, let's meet Him in His Word . . . in prayer . . . in worship.

Read Psalm 143.

god's judgment

It was the old country preacher, Vance Havner, who once said, "If God dealt with people today as He did in the days of Ananias and Sapphira, every church would need a morgue in the basement."

That statement makes a lot of people smile. Not me. It makes me think . . . and wonder why. Actually, I've got several "why" questions when it comes to God's judgment. Why isn't His judgment more obvious in the lives of those who willfully and deliberately disobey? Why doesn't He act swiftly and severely since His holiness is being smeared and His reputation is at stake? Why won't He make His promise good every time we resist paying back evil for evil . . . especially since He repeats that promise so often in Scripture, "Vengeance is Mine, I will repay," says the Lord (Deuteronomy 32:35; Romans 12:17-19; Hebrews 10:30).

That reference in Hebrews even concludes, "The Lord will judge His people." Forgive me if I seem cruelly severe, but my concern is *when*? Where are the Ananias-and-Sapphira examples today when Christians deceive other Christians? Why aren't more among us weak and ill . . . and why don't more actually die(!) as they did in the Corinthian assembly when they failed to take God seriously (1 Corinthians 11:30)? If Ananias and Sapphira couldn't get the Lord to overlook even one solitary act of hypocrisy, how come today some can lie, cheat, steal, and sleep around, then go right on as if it were business as usual? And while we're at it, if 1 Corinthians 5:11 is indeed part of Scripture, what makes us hesitant to *do* what it says?

> . . . I wrote to you not to associate with any so-called brother if he should be an immoral person, or covetous, or an idolater, or a reviler, or a drunkard, or a swindler—not even to eat with such a one.

Yes, that's a direct quote . . . in context . . . correctly translated from the Greek text. I checked. If it means anything, it means this: Isolation is one of the consequences when a believer adopts an unbiblical lifestyle. Taken literally, that means *everyone* who names the name of Christ should refuse to take the edge off the carnal Christian's loneliness. Even family members are to cooperate with the divinely ordered isolation until there is repentance.

Paul's implication is this (contrary to popular opinion): By refusing to associate or eat with those who live compromising, irresponsible, immoral lives, God's judgment—divine vengeance—will then occur. We can count on it! Ah, but *there's* the rub. Often, it seems, it doesn't. I can state case after case where God's judgment never did fall. And frankly, I'm struggling with that. If He is holy (I know He is) and if He hates sin (I know He does) and if He is jealous that His Church be a pure Bride (yes, that's true, too), *where is the proof*? To be painfully specific, why can one Christian after another walk away from his or her marriage with scarcely a hint of overt divine vengeance? Or how can believers decide that a homosexual lifestyle is acceptable, then start to practice it without suffering a similar judgment as that which fell on the sodomites who lived in the ancient twin cities, Sodom and Gomorrah? Was it wrong then but okay now?

I know the heavenly answer to those questions, but where is the earthly proof? Surely God knows that the absence of divine discipline is being used against Him! And that makes me mad. And sad. And a little confused. Especially when I am dealing with marital infidelity and the mate who was faithful (and did everything possible to make the marriage work) looks at me and sincerely asks, "Why does the Lord let my partner get away with that?" The Lord leaves a lot of us wondering, not just those trying to pick up the pieces.

With my whole heart I agree with the psalmist, "It is time for the Lord to act, for they have broken Thy law" (Psalm 119:126). I believe that if He were to act as decisively as He did so often in biblical times, marvelous changes would sweep across Christendom. A healthy fear of the Lord would again grip His people as respect for His holy name returned. An obedient walk would become evident among us. Furthermore, a renewed determination to uphold one's marital vows would solidify homes. And a purer Bride, with genuine, priceless character, would await the arrival of her Groom.

Is it not time to pray more boldly and fervently? Is it not appropriate that we stand squarely on Peter's warning, ". . . it is time for judgment to begin with the household of God . . ." (1 Peter 4:17)? Yes, I think so. In fact, I see every reason that we ask our Lord to act swiftly, severely if necessary, and significantly enough to grab everyone's attention, including those right now toying with the idea of drifting away.

I read this past week of a couple (let's call them Carl and Clara) whose twenty-five year marriage was a good one. Not the most idyllic, but good. They now had three grown children who loved them dearly. They were also blessed with sufficient financial security to allow them room to dream about a lakeside retirement home. They began looking. A widower we'll call Ben was selling his place. They liked it a lot and returned home to talk and plan. Months passed.

Last fall, right out of the blue, Clara told Carl she wanted a divorce. He went numb. After all these years, why? And how could she deceive him . . . how could she have been nursing such a scheme while they were looking at a retirement home? She said she hadn't been. Actually, this was a recent decision now that she had found another man. Who? Clara admitted it was Ben, the owner of the lake house, whom she inadvertently ran into several weeks after they had discussed the sale. They'd begun seeing each other. Since they were now "in love," there was no turning back. Not even the kids, who hated the idea, could dissuade their mother.

On the day she was to leave, Carl walked through the kitchen toward the garage. Realizing she would be gone when he returned, he hesitated, "Well, hon, I guess this is the last time—" His voice dissolved as he broke into sobs. She felt uneasy, hurriedly got her things together, and drove north to join Ben. Less than two weeks after she moved in with Ben, her new lover, he was seized with a heart attack. He lingered a few hours . . . and then died.

It is time for our holy God to act. Yes, *that* significantly.

In a depraved world, it is difficult to find many sources of encouragement and happiness. Look around. The scene is bleak and grim. Corruption, oppression, infidelity, injustice, and rivalry await us around most corners, breeding discouragement and fear. So it is "around" us . . . under the sun . . . but never "above" us. May God give us eyes to see through our circumstances and to hear His voice of reassurance through the cracks and crevices along this journey called life. As we seek Him this day, may new insights bring fresh encouragement, new sounds, and long overdue happiness. Don't miss the sights. Listen carefully.

Read Hebrews 12.

doormats

My heart goes out to those who live their lives like whipped dogs. You've seen them, too. They are stooped, shy, reluctant, and fearful. It's as if they were carrying the weight of the world on their shoulders. They may be gifted, gracious people, but their inability to project the slightest degree of confidence keeps their competence a well-hidden secret.

David Seamands writes of such a man:

> . . . Ben was one of the most timid souls I have ever counseled. I couldn't even hear him. "What did you say, Ben?" We began practicing to raise Ben's voice. I would have him read things to me. "A little louder, Ben. Assert yourself. Speak up!" He was so afraid to be a burden to people. It could make a person uncomfortable to be around him. You might look to see if he was wearing a sandwich board that read, "Excuse me for living."

> Have you ever heard of the "Dependent Order of Really Meek and Timid Souls"? When you make an acrostic of its first letters, you have "Doormats." The Doormats have an official insignia—a yellow caution light. Their official motto is: "The meek shall inherit the earth, if that's OK with everybody!" The society was founded by Upton Dickson who wrote a pamphlet called *Cower Power*. Well, Ben could have been a charter member of the Doormats.[9]

Dr. Seamands goes on to describe the arduous process Ben struggled through in order to overcome his whipped-dog lifestyle. Thanks to an extended period of time spent with several accepting and affirming friends, the young man was able to unload his story, which included a series of painful memories. Perhaps the most difficult of all was the feeling that he had been the cause of his mother's nervous breakdown . . . of her being an emotional invalid. If you can believe it, Ben had actually been told that by others while he was a young teenager. Without being consciously aware of it, he was living under an enormous load of guilt brought about by that cruel and unjust accusation. When he finally forced himself to declare his anguish, Ben sobbed with release. Within a relatively brief period of time, the gigantic weight slipped from his shoulders and he was able to put a stop to the inner penance he had lived with for years.

How much hurt, how much damage can be done by chance remarks! Our unguarded tongues can deposit germ-thoughts of hurt, humiliation, and hate into tender minds which fester, become full-blown infections, and ultimately spread disease throughout an adult personality. With little regard for the other person's vulnerability, we have the power to initiate a violent emotional earthquake by merely making a few statements that rip and tear like shrapnel in the person's head. Such destructive words are like sending 800 volts through 110 wire.

But the surprising reaction is an out-of-balance timidity rather than overt rage. It isn't that anger and resentment and hate are absent. On the contrary! It's that all those feelings are buried beneath layers of timidity, meekness, and, yes, even spiritual-sounding piety. It's easy to be fooled by Doormats who have developed ways to mask their pain . . . especially since Christians are much more comfortable around "sit-down-and-stay-quiet" types than "stand-up-and-say-it-straight" types.

I find help in Solomon's proverbs. He mentions "tongue," "lips," "mouth," and "words" a little less than 150 times—that's just under 5 times a chapter. Over and over he exhorts us to watch what we say, when we say it, and how we say it. Offense or healing can come from the same throat. Furthermore, the wise man warns us against masking the truth . . . and thinking that quietness always means peacefulness. And on and on and on.

May I offer a suggestion for your quest for character during the next month? Proverbs has thirty-one chapters. How about reading a chapter a day? Wisdom is waiting, I can assure you.

And who knows? We may gain enough insight to realize that whipped dogs are sometimes mad dogs, ready to bite . . . and dependent souls are often diseased souls, needing to be healed.

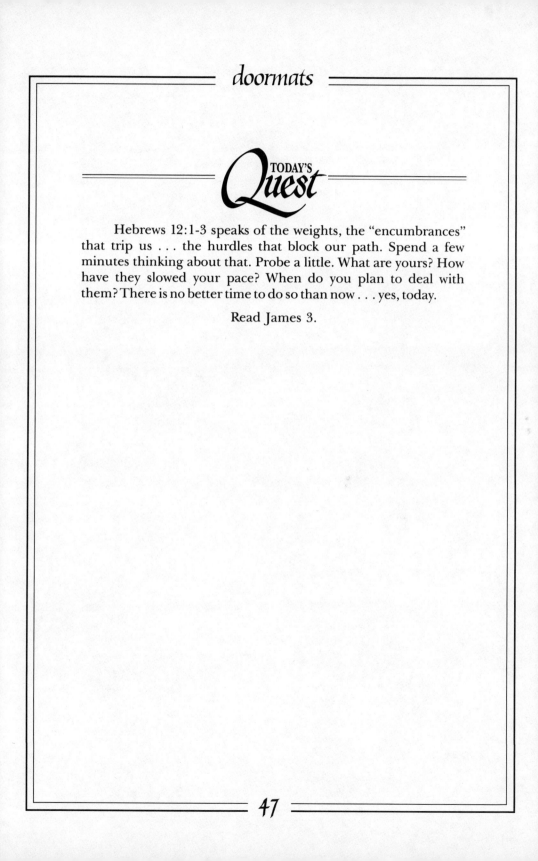

TODAY'S *Quest*

Hebrews 12:1-3 speaks of the weights, the "encumbrances" that trip us . . . the hurdles that block our path. Spend a few minutes thinking about that. Probe a little. What are yours? How have they slowed your pace? When do you plan to deal with them? There is no better time to do so than now . . . yes, today.

Read James 3.

SOW A THOUGHT,
REAP AN ACT;
SOW AN ACT,
REAP A HABIT;
SOW A HABIT,
REAP A CHARACTER;
SOW A CHARACTER,
REAP A DESTINY.

restoration

When the twelve returned from a busy time of public ministry, they gave their reports and told Jesus all they had done and taught (Mark 6:30). I think it is extremely significant that our Lord *did not* push them right back into action or hurry them on to another assignment. Matter of fact, we never read that He "rushed" anywhere. Not on your life!

> He said to them, "Come away by yourselves to a lonely place and rest a while." (For there were many people coming and going, and they did not even have time to eat.) And they went away in the boat to a lonely place by themselves (Mark 6:31-32).

Renewal and restoration are not luxuries; they are essentials. Being alone and resting for a while is not selfish; it is Christlike. Taking your day off each week or rewarding yourself with a relaxing, refreshing vacation is not carnal; it's spiritual. There is absolutely nothing enviable or spiritual about a coronary or a nervous breakdown, nor is an ultrabusy schedule necessarily the mark of a productive life. I often remind myself of the ancient Greek motto, "You will break the bow if you keep it always bent."

Well . . . how's it going in *your* life? Let's take a brief appraisal. Pause long enough to review and reflect. Try to be honest as you answer these questions. They may hurt a little.

- Is my pace this year really that different from last year?
- Am I enjoying most of my activities or just enduring them?
- Have I deliberately taken time on several occasions this year for personal restoration?
- Are my meals choked down or do I take sufficient time to taste and enjoy my food?
- Do I give myself permission to relax, to have leisure, to be quiet?
- Would other people think I am working too many hours and/or living under too much stress? Am I occasionally boring and often preoccupied?
- Am I staying physically fit? Do I consider my body important enough to maintain a nourishing diet, to give it regular exercise, to get enough sleep, to shed those excess pounds?
- How is my sense of humor?
- Is God being glorified by the schedule I keep . . . or is He getting the leftovers of my energy?
- Am I getting dangerously close to "burnout"?

Tough stuff, huh? Yet what better time than *right now* to do a little evaluating . . . and, if necessary, some restructuring of our lives. We can learn a lesson from nature. A period of rest always follows a harvest; the land must be allowed time to renew itself. Constant production without restoration depletes resources and, in fact, diminishes the quality of what is produced.

Superachievers and workaholics, take heed! If the light on your inner dashboard is flashing red, you are carrying too much too far too fast. If you don't pull over, you'll be sorry . . . and so will all those who love you. If you are courageous enough to get out of that fast lane and make some needed changes, you will show yourself wise. But I should warn you of three barriers you will immediately face.

First, *false guilt*. By saying no to the people to whom you used to say yes, you'll feel twinges of guilt. Ignore it! Second, *hostility and misunderstanding* from others. Most folks won't understand your new decisions or your slower pace, especially those who are in the sinking boat you just stepped out of. No problem. Stick by your guns. Third, you'll encounter some *personal and painful insights*. By not filling every spare moment with another activity, you will begin to see the real you, and you'll not like some of those things you observe, things that once contaminated your busy life. But within a relatively brief period of time, you will turn the corner and be well on the road to a happier, healthier, freer, and more fulfilling life. Furthermore, your quest for character will get back on track.

Obviously, all this stuff on rest and renewal, taking some time off and relaxing, can be taken to a ridiculous extreme. I'm well aware of that. But for every person who will gravitate to that extreme and rust out, there are thousands more of us who have a much greater battle with burnout. Neither extreme is correct—either way, we're "out."

My desire is that all of us remain "in." In balance. In our right minds. In good health. In the will of God.

Are you?

This moment of quiet reflection is what David had in mind when he wrote of "green pastures" and "still waters." Drink in the stillness! Linger as long as you can in the presence of your loving Shepherd. His word will restore you as "the paths of righteousness" become clear. Even if this day is shadowed by fear or uncertainty, He is *with* you . . . as close as your heartbeat, as close as your next breath. Sing your praise to Him! The worship of God anoints our days and causes dry cups to overflow.

Read Psalm 23.

that day...this day

For the next few minutes, imagine this scene:

But the day of the Lord will come like a thief, in which the heavens will pass away with a roar and the elements will be destroyed with intense heat, and the earth and its works will be burned up. Since all these things are to be destroyed in this way, what sort of people ought you to be in holy conduct and godliness, looking for . . . the coming of the day of God, on account of which the heavens will be destroyed by burning, and the elements will melt with intense heat! (2 Peter 3:10-12).

Scary stuff, that business about the heavens passing away and the astronomical destruction and the twice-mentioned "intense heat" that will result in a total wipeout of Planet Earth. Makes me wonder *how*. Always has. I've heard the same things you have about superatomic warheads and nuclear missiles in World War III. But somehow that never explained how "the heavens will pass away" or how the surrounding atmosphere and stratosphere could be "destroyed by burning."

Since that would usher in "the day of God," I've always had reservations that He would use men's fireworks to announce His arrival. If I read these verses correctly, they describe such phenomenal destructive force it would make our armory of demolition devices look like a two-bit cherry bomb under a tin can. It's impossible to imagine!

But in my reading several years ago, I stumbled across a possible breakthrough. It may be a hint on how the Lord might be planning to pull off this final blast.

On March 9, 1979, nine satellites stationed at various points in the solar system simultaneously recorded a bizarre event deep in space. It was, in fact, *the most powerful burst of energy ever recorded*. Astronomers who studied the readings were awestruck, mumbling to themselves.

The burst of gamma radiation lasted for only one-tenth of a second . . . but in that instant it emitted as much energy as the sun does in 3,000 years. An astrophysicist named Doyle Evans, who works at the Los Alamos Scientific Laboratories in New Mexico, said the energy being emitted was at a rate of 100 billion times greater than the energy emission rate of the sun. If the gamma-ray burst had occurred in the Milky Way galaxy, it would have set our entire atmosphere aglow. If the sun had suddenly emitted the same amount of energy, our earth would have vaporized. Instantly.

There's more. The satellites were able to pinpoint the location of the burst to a spot in a galaxy known as N-49, which is associated with the remnants of a supernova believed to have exploded about ten thousand years ago. When a star explodes into a supernova, the outer shell is blown away and the inner core condenses from its own gravity to create a neutron star. That core becomes a single, huge nucleus, shrinking from a size larger than the sun (860,000 miles in diameter) to a compact ball no more than five miles across. Those neutrons are so incredibly dense that one cubic inch weighs 20 million, million pounds. Many astronomers believe the satellite studies will open up a new understanding of neutron stars and other objects in the heavens.

The earth's atmosphere previously had prevented astronomers from studying gamma radiation. Only in recent years has a network of satellites equipped with gamma-ray detectors enabled scientists to locate the sources of gamma rays.

As untrained and ignorant as we may be of the technical side of all this, I suggest it might cast some light on the validity of Peter's remark. At least, in my estimation, it makes a lot more sense than atomic wars. It's probably going to be more like the ultimate *Star Wars*—and I have no plans to be around at the premier showing.

But let's not overlook Peter's piercing question in verse 11. Facing an imminent execution, the old fisherman lifts his weathered face and looks across the centuries at you and me. Can you feel his gaze? Can you see the concern etched in deep lines around his eyes? Can you hear his gravelly voice?

"Since all these things are to be destroyed in this way, *what sort of people ought you to be . . . ?*"

Since the world and all its works will one day dissolve in one convulsive flash, what kind of life ought we to be living on this temporary, soon-to-pass world? What kind of priorities ought to shape our schedules? What kind of considerations ought to map our steps, guide our conversations, and determine our direction?

"What sort of people ought you to be?" It's a question regarding our character.

Peter answers his own question in the next gasp.

Surely men of good and holy character, who live expecting and working for the coming day of God (3:11, Phillips).

That day, says Peter, should have an impact on *this* day. Guard your heart from anything that might cause you embarrassment when *that* day arrives.

"For the eyes of the Lord move to and fro throughout the earth that He may strongly support those whose heart is completely His" (2 Chronicles 16:9). Many things occur when we set our hearts to seek God, including *personal* evaluation. Is your heart "completely His"? Choose one area of reservation and invite the Spirit of God to break through, to dig in, to conquer new ground. Turn your prayers today in the direction of surrender rather than defense. He will "strongly support" that attitude. Release!

Read 2 Peter 3.

single-mindedness

James doesn't mess around. He goes for the jugular with a sharp bayonet. Right up front he warns us against being "double-minded." He tells us that when we are, we become "unstable in all our ways." Shaky. In today's terms, we begin to bear the marks of a flake.

Double-mindedness is a common disease that leaves its victims paralyzed by doubt . . . hesitant, hypocritical, full of theoretical words, but lacking in confident action. Lots of talk but no guts. Insincere and insecure. Again, James says it best: ". . . let not that man expect that he will receive anything from the Lord." Jab, twist. Like I say, James doesn't mess around.

I suggest we take this passage literally. "Unstable" means unstable. "Driven and tossed" means driven and tossed. Not receiving "anything" means just that. God deliberately holds back when the double-minded person prays. I call that serious.

How much better to be single-minded! No mumbo-jumbo. No religious phony-baloney. No say-one-thing-but-mean-something-else jive. No pharisaic hypocrisy where words come cheap and externals are sickeningly pious. The single-minded are short on creeds and long on deeds.

They care . . . *really* care. They are humble . . . *truly* humble. They love . . . *genuinely* love. They have character . . . *authentic* character.

Lord of reality
make me real
not plastic
synthetic
pretend phony
an actor playing out his part
hypocrite.
I don't want
to keep a prayer list
but to pray
nor agonize to find Your will
but to obey
what I already know
to argue
theories of inspiration
but submit to Your Word.
I don't want
to explain the difference
between eros and philos
and agape
but to love.
I don't want
to sing as if I mean it
I want to mean it.
I don't want
to tell it like it is
but to be it
like you want it.

I don't want
to think another needs me
but I need him
else I'm not complete.
I don't want
to tell others how to do it
but to do it
to have to be always right
but to admit it when I'm wrong.
I don't want to be a census taker
but an obstetrician
nor an involved person, a professional
but a friend
I don't want to be insensitive
but to hurt where other people hurt
nor to say I know how you feel
but to say God knows
and I'll try
if you'll be patient with me
and meanwhile I'll be quiet.
I don't want to scorn the clichés of others
but to mean everything I say
including this.[10]

Appropriately, Joe Bayly called that prayer "A Psalm of Single-mindedness." God doesn't hold back from a prayer like that because Joe didn't say one thing and mean something else. Like James, Joe didn't mess around with what he said. He's gone from this earth now, but his words live on. He was like someone else I know.

His name is *Jesus*.

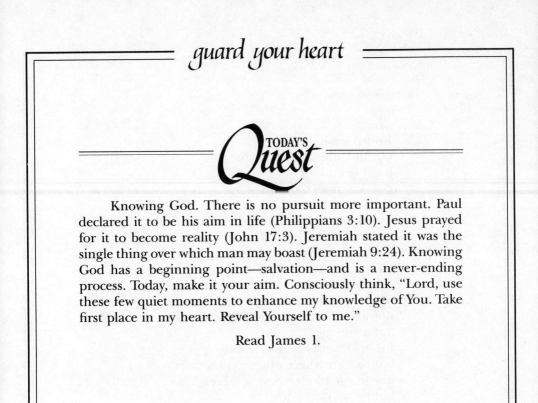

TODAY'S
Quest

Knowing God. There is no pursuit more important. Paul declared it to be his aim in life (Philippians 3:10). Jesus prayed for it to become reality (John 17:3). Jeremiah stated it was the single thing over which man may boast (Jeremiah 9:24). Knowing God has a beginning point—salvation—and is a never-ending process. Today, make it your aim. Consciously think, "Lord, use these few quiet moments to enhance my knowledge of You. Take first place in my heart. Reveal Yourself to me."

Read James 1.

loneliness in leadership

There are times my heart really goes out to our President. Not only does he have the toughest job in the world, in addition to that he cannot win, no matter what he decides. Since doves and hawks will never coexist, there is no way he'll ever get them in the same cage together. There must be times when he begins to doubt his own value . . . times when he hears the footsteps of his critics and wonders if they may be right. The Oval Office has to be the loneliest place in America. The only comfort the man has is that *he is not unique*. Every President who preceded him experienced similar struggles. Being the Chief includes that occupational hazard.

I was reminded of this recently when I read of a television program aired on PBS on that most staid of subjects—a library. This, however, was the Library of Congress, and the PBS's former chairman, Sir Huw Wheldon, was standing in a forest of card index files. The program had all the makings of a slow-moving, dull documentary until . . .

About halfway through, Dr. Daniel Boorstin, the Librarian of Congress, brought out a little blue box from a small closet that once held the library's rarities.

The label on the box read: CONTENTS OF THE PRESIDENT'S POCKETS ON THE NIGHT OF APRIL 14, 1865.

Since that was the fateful night Abraham Lincoln was assassinated, every viewer's attention was seized.

Boorstin then proceeded to remove the items in the small container and display them on camera. There were five things in the box:

- A handkerchief, embroidered "A. Lincoln"
- A country boy's pen knife
- A spectacles case repaired with string
- A purse containing a $5 bill—*Confederate money*(!)
- Some old and worn newspaper clippings

"The clippings," said Boorstin, "were concerned with the great deeds of Abraham Lincoln. And one of them actually reports a speech by John Bright which says that Abraham Lincoln is "one of the greatest men of all times."

Today, that's common knowledge. The world now knows that British statesman John Bright was right in his assessment of Lincoln, but in 1865 millions shared quite a contrary opinion. The President's critics were fierce and many. His was a lonely agony that reflected the suffering and turmoil of his country ripped to shreds by hatred and a cruel, costly war.

There is something touchingly pathetic in the mental picture of this great leader seeking solace and self-assurance from a few old newspaper clippings as he reads them under the flickering flame of a candle all alone in the Oval Office.

Remember this: Loneliness stalks where the buck stops.

In the final analysis, top leaders pay a high price for their position. Think of some examples. Moses had no close chums. Nor did Joshua. You find David with Jonathan only in his earlier years—but when he became the monarch of Israel, his greatest battles, his deepest prayers, his hardest decisions occurred in solitude. The same with Daniel. And the other prophets? Loneliest men in the Old Testament. Paul frequently wrote of this in his letters. He informed his understudy, Timothy:

> ... *everyone in the province of Asia has deserted me* (2 Timothy 1:15, NIV).

Ever thought about evangelist Billy Graham's life *apart from* his crusades and periodic public appearances? Or the president of a Christian organization or educational institution? Do that for a moment or two. They would qualify as illustrations of A. W. Tozer's statement: *"Most of the world's great souls have been lonely."*

Now don't misread this. It's not that the leader is aloof and unaccountable or purposely withdrawing or has something to hide—it's just the nature of the role. It is in lonely solitude that God delivers His best thoughts, and the mind needs to be still and quiet to receive them. And much of the weight of the office simply cannot be borne by others. Mystical though it may sound, it is absolutely essential that those whom God appoints to places of leadership learn to breathe comfortably in the thin air of the Himalayan heights where God's comfort and assurance come in the crushing silence of solitude. Where man's opinion is overshadowed. Where faith replaces fear. Where the quest for character deepens. Where (as F. B. Meyer once put it) vision clears as the silt drops from the current of our life.

It is there, alone and apart, true leaders earn the right to be respected. And learn the full meaning of those profound words, "Be still and know that I am God."

In every life
   There's a pause that is better than onward rush,
   Better than hewing or mightiest doing;
   'Tis the standing still at Sovereign will.

   There's a hush that is better than ardent speech,
   Better than sighing or wilderness crying;
   'Tis the being still at Sovereign will.

The pause and the hush sing a double song
In unison low and for all time long.
O human soul, God's working plan
Goes on, nor needs the aid of man!
   Stand still and see!
   Be still and know![11]

Read Psalm 46.

sincerity

"Angela Atwood was a dear, honest, sincere girl, who—
like Christ—died for her beliefs."

Those words actually fell from the lips of a Roman
Catholic priest as he delivered Angela's eulogy to those
who had gathered in St. Paul's Church of Prospect
Park, New Jersey. Since the events surrounding
Angela's death have faded into the sordid history of
America's radical era, let me jog your memory. This
young woman was one of six hard-core gang members
who called themselves the "Symbionese Liberation
Army." She and her companions were killed in a fiery
shoot-out with law enforcement authorities in Los
Angeles back in the seventies.

"This *sincere* girl was following a Christian voca-
tion," said the priest, because she, like Christ, was willing to die for what she *sincerely* believed in. Although
a vicious outlaw, a fugitive trained in the grim art of
murder, Angela's *sincerity* supposedly cleared her of
blame and (if you dare believe it) linked her to Christ.

"Sincerity" is considered the international credit
card of acceptance. Flash it in the face of Mr. and Mrs.
Gullible Public and it will be honored without question.

No matter how deeply in debt the user may be or how the card is misused, "sincerity" will erase all suspicion and validate all actions. You don't even need to sign the voucher. Just write "I'm sincere" at the end of each transaction and you'll become another in a long line of card-carrying creatures who keep our world on the edge of crisis. For some strange reason justice sleeps as judge and jury smile at the ultimate verdict: "Not guilty . . . because of sincerity."

Since when does "sincerity" grant me the right to do wrong? Charles Whitman was *sincere* when he carried his portable armory atop the observation tower at the University of Texas and picked off sixteen innocent passersby. The young Arab terrorist was *sincere* when he drove his carload of explosives into the Marine barracks in Beruit, killing 241 young American peacekeepers. So was Sirhan Sirhan when he murdered Senator Robert Kennedy . . . and Adolph Hitler when he wrote *Mein-Kampf* . . . and Benedict Arnold when he betrayed his country on the banks of the Hudson . . . and Judas when he sold his soul for silver.

Sure they were sincere. But they were sincerely *wrong*. No amount of devotion or determination or sacrificial involvement in wrong actions will ever make them right. Shouting louder doesn't make a weak argument strong. Driving faster doesn't help when you're lost. Adding more signatures doesn't make a phony college degree respectable. So then—neither does sincerity excuse sin, regardless of what some misguided, well-meaning clergyman may say at a funeral.

But does this mean that sincerity is questionable? Not really. It might be better to say that the value of sincerity depends on what it represents. In his letter to the Philippian believers, Paul prays that their love

. . . may abound still more and more in real knowledge and all discernment, so that you may approve the things that are excellent, in order to be sincere and blameless until the day of Christ (Philippians 1:9-10).

We who are on a quest for character must allow sincerity to be our badge of excellence throughout our days on earth. *Sincere* is actually a Latin word, meaning "without wax." The Greek term means "sun-tested." You see, the ancients had a very fine porcelain which was greatly valued and therefore expensive. Often when fired in the kiln tiny cracks would appear. Dishonest merchants would smear pearly-white wax over these cracks, which would pass for true porcelain—unless held up to the light of the sun. Honest dealers marked their flawless wares *sine cera*— "without wax."

And that is genuine sincerity. No sham, no hypocrisy. No hidden cracks to be covered over. When true sincerity flows from our lives, things that are excellent are approved, to paraphrase Paul's point. We are *then* (and only then) "like Christ."

When the Son shines through and tests our lives, the absence of cracks will guarantee the presence of truth. You cannot separate the two . . . no matter how sincere you may be.

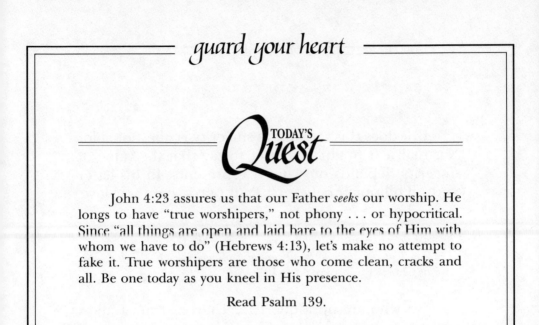

TODAY'S
Quest

John 4:23 assures us that our Father *seeks* our worship. He longs to have "true worshipers," not phony . . . or hypocritical. Since "all things are open and laid bare to the eyes of Him with whom we have to do" (Hebrews 4:13), let's make no attempt to fake it. True worshipers are those who come clean, cracks and all. Be one today as you kneel in His presence.

Read Psalm 139.

honesty

SHOPLIFTERS WILL BE PROSECUTED TO THE
FULL EXTENT OF THE LAW.

•

SHOPLIFTING IS STEALING. STOP IT!

•

ALL MERCHANDISE IN THIS STORE IS MORE
EXPENSIVE NOW THAN EVER BECAUSE OF
SHOPLIFTING. HELP US FIGHT INFLATION.
STOP SHOPLIFTING.

•

SHOPLIFTERS . . . DON'T!

I counted a dozen such signs in the same store yesterday. The shelves had been completely rearranged and the front door bolted shut permanently, forcing all customers to enter and exit inconveniently through a narrow aisle near the rear door by the cash register.

Why? Dishonesty. The manager confessed:

> We were getting ripped off, frankly. Children, mothers, businessmen, blue collar workers . . . professionals . . . you name it! Some shelves were stripped bare by closing time.

Last week I read about a woman, apparently pregnant, who walked out of the grocery store. Suspicious, the assistant manager stopped her. She later "gave birth" to a pound of butter, a chuck roast, a bottle of pancake syrup, two tubes of toothpaste, hair tonic, and several bars of candy. One California homemaker was observed tapping various articles as she made her way through a supermarket, followed by her two children who quickly pocketed the designated items. Sophisticated alarm systems, one-way mirrors, locking devices, moving cameras, and electronic tape signals work hard at monitoring and exposing the problem . . . but it only grows larger. One estimate says that one out of every fifty-two customers every day carries away at least one unpaid-for item. The loss as of this writing is now an astronomical $3 billion annually . . . and rising.

Now let's remember that shoplifting is merely one thin slice of humanity's stale cake of dishonesty. Don't forget our depraved track record: cheating on exams, taking a towel from the hotel, not working a full eight hours, bold-face lies and half truths, exaggerated statements, hedging on reports of losses covered by insurance companies, broken financial promises, domestic deceit, and (dare I mention) ye olde I.R.S. reports we *sign* as being the truth. Did you know that ever since 1811 (when someone who had defrauded the government anonymously sent $5 to Washington D.C.) the U.S. Treasury has operated a *Conscience Fund*? Since that time almost $3.5 million has been received from guilt-ridden citizens.

The answer, simplistic though it may seem, is a return to honesty. Integrity may be an even better word. It would be a tough reversal for some . . . but oh, how needed! It boils down to an internal decision. Nothing less will counteract dishonesty. External punishment may hurt, but it doesn't solve. It's my understanding that in some Arab communities when they catch a man stealing, they cut off his hand. You might think that would be sufficient to curb national dishonesty. But from what we read, it could hardly be said the Arabs have any corner on integrity.

Cutting off a hand to stop stealing misses the heart of the problem by about twenty-four inches. Dishonesty doesn't start in the hand any more than greed starts in the eye. It's an internal disease. It reveals a serious character flaw.

Ideally, we plant the seeds and cultivate the roots of honesty in the *home*. Under the watchful eyes of consistent, diligent, persistent parents! In the best laboratory of life God ever designed—the family unit. It is *there* a proper scale of values is imbibed as the worth of a dollar is learned. It is on that anvil that the appreciation for hard work, the esteem for truth, the reward for achievement, and the cost of dishonesty are hammered out so that a life is shaped correctly down deep inside. Down where character is forged.

But what if you weren't so trained? Is there any hope?

Certainly! One of the reasons Christianity is so appealing is the hope it provides. Christ doesn't offer a technique on rebuilding *your* life. He offers you *His* life—His honesty, His integrity. Not a lot of rules and don'ts and threats. But sufficient power to counteract your dishonest bent. He calls it "a new nature, pure and undefiled . . . ." Thoroughly honest. Some would tell you that believing in Jesus Christ—trusting Him to break old habits and make you honest—means cutting off your head. Committing intellectual suicide. Is operating your inner life on the faith principle (instead of failure) wishful thinking? No way! It is not only the best way to stop being dishonest, it's the *only* way.

You need cut off neither your hand nor your head to become an honest person. What you want to cut off is your *habit*, by allowing Christ to be the honored Presence throughout your inner home.

It won't be long before you find that honesty is the Guest policy.

Alive. Active. Penetrating. Powerful. That's God's Word. Unlike anything else that has ever been written, Scripture touches hearts and changes lives. Today, as always, we need His touch. Painful and deep though it may be, His surgery inevitably benefits us. May His Spirit prepare our hearts for the probing ministry of the two-edged sword.

Read Hebrews 4:12-16.

yesterday, today, tomorrow

One of my long-time friends, Tom Craik, makes his living working as a high school counselor. He's committed to strengthening family relationships, especially helping moms, dads, and kids learn to love each other—which includes accepting, respecting, and communicating with one another.

For years, Tom has been in touch with the full spectrum of families in turmoil, so there is not much he hasn't seen or heard. He has never failed to shoot straight with me, a trait I greatly admire. He recently mailed me some musings that I might wish to share with others. Because they are related to true character development in the home, they caught my attention.

> With school having started again, we are probably all aware of what ways we are going to be different this school year. We are going to be different kids this year. We are going to work harder at our studies. This year we'll get A's and B's, be more respectful to our folks, show good sense in all our endeavors so that we will be seen as responsible young adults.
>
> This year we are going to be more of a family, we are going to be more together, enjoy each other's company more. We are going to like to be with each other. Maybe

we'll even go on some weekend outings. As a family we'll argue less and discuss more. We'll respect each other's opinions and talk in a civilized, grown-up, positive, and loving way. We will eat meals together and find out how everyone's day went and really support each other.

This year Dad will stop drinking and Mom won't yell so much. This year my brothers and sisters will all get along better. We'll help each other with our studies and help Mom around the house. This year Mom and Dad won't have to keep bugging us to do our chores; we'll just do them. We'll keep our rooms clean and put the dishes in the dishwasher. No fights and hassles for us this year. This year we'll appreciate Mom and Dad more because now we really do know all of what they do for us. I can hear it now: "This year I'll be able to go to bed at night and not have to worry about Mom's and Dad's fighting because this year things are going to be different. Because this year I'm going to do better so Mom and Dad won't have any reason to scream and drink and fight. One thing's for sure, we're all going to get along better this year."

Any of this sound even vaguely familiar? Most likely though, by the time you read this, these "dreams" are going to be history as yesterday becomes today . . . becomes tomorrow.

I'm thirty-one years old next month. When I divide that by two, I'm fifteen and a half. Believe it or not, that was just yesterday. Double it and I'm sixty-two. Believe it or not, I think that's tomorrow. Sometime yesterday morning my son was born. Today he's almost a year old. Tomorrow he'll be fifteen. Where does it all go? What's happened to the "dreams"? And you know something else? I know less today than I did yesterday and probably more now than I will know tomorrow. Zoom! There it goes. There I go!

Parents, most of this applies to us. We are the ones who create the atmosphere, the climate in our homes. We create the tension or the peace, the conflict or the order. We choose whether our homes are loving and supportive or hateful and isolating. We are the ones who teach self-responsibility or blame. We are the ones who look for the good or complain, complain, complain.

Kids, tomorrow you're going to be thirty. The time is already past to look for someone to blame, to look for some reason why things aren't the way you want them to be. Create your own change. Take care of yourself. Act in your own best interest. Work at seeing what you want for yourself and then go about getting it. Find your intention, your purpose, your dream and realize that if it is going to happen, you're the one who's got to make it happen. And then go to it!

Gotta go. My son's looking for the car keys....[12]

Tom's right. Painfully right.

Instead of just reading these words, or simply thinking them over, how about our taking the man's advice? The secret lies in how we handle today, not yesterday or tomorrow. *Today* . . . that special block of time holding the key that locks out yesterday's nightmares and unlocks tomorrow's dreams.

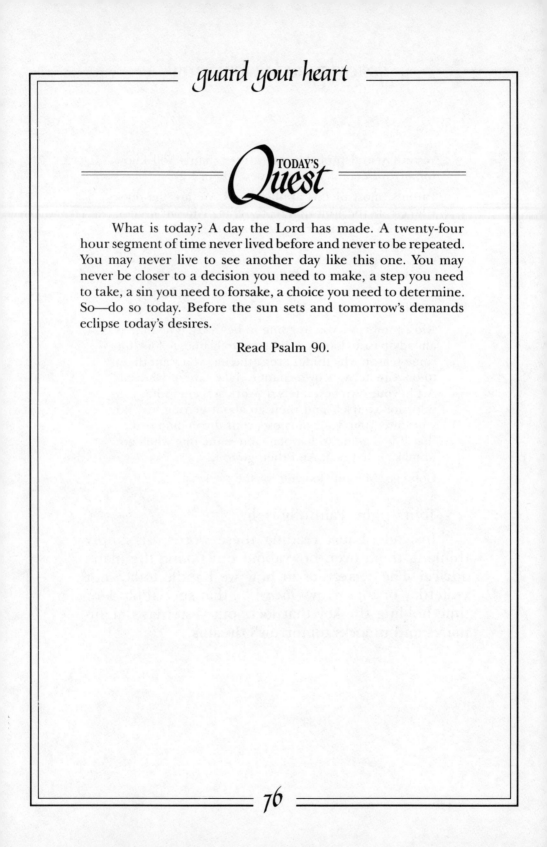

TODAY'S Quest

What is today? A day the Lord has made. A twenty-four hour segment of time never lived before and never to be repeated. You may never live to see another day like this one. You may never be closer to a decision you need to make, a step you need to take, a sin you need to forsake, a choice you need to determine. So—do so today. Before the sun sets and tomorrow's demands eclipse today's desires.

Read Psalm 90.

feast and famine

During the reign of Queen Victoria, the United Kingdom was neck deep in biblical truth. A sumptuous feast was served each Lord's Day and one could take his pick without fear of ever going hungry. No one wept over the lack of spiritual food. Here's why.

- Charles Haddon Spurgeon was wielding the Sword at the Metropolitan Tabernacle in London.
- Not too far from there, a congregation of 3,000 at the City Temple was well-nourished for thirty-three years under Joseph Parker's ministry.
- The saintly F. B. Meyer was leading people into a closer, more meaningful walk with God.
- William Booth was thundering against the sins of the city.
- C. H. Liddon was at St. Paul's, standing firm.
- Dr. Alexander MacLaren was delivering some of the finest expository messages in the history of the church.
- R. W. Dale was in Birmingham, holding forth for thirty-six years at Carr's Lane. Two years before his death, G. Campbell Morgan began his pastorate at the nearby Westminster Road Congregational Church in the same city.

- Alexander Whyte was then an associate alongside the famous Robert S. Candlish at Free St. George's in Edinburgh. He later succeeded his godly mentor, remaining a total of forty-seven years in that one church ministering to multiple thousands of Scottish saints.
- And we must not forget the somewhat frequent visits of American evangelist Dwight L. Moody, who could be heard in a dozen or more cities of Great Britain during that same remarkable period of time.

What an epochal era! There were giants in the land in those days and their immensity cast an array of impressive shadows across the landscape of Christendom as at no other time in the illustrious history of the Isles. They personified the second stanza of that grand gospel song written in their day:

> *Like a mighty army,*
> *moves the church of God* . . . .[13]

But the cadence is now muffled. That once-strong army of valiant and vigorous soldiers seems strangely reduced to mere squads here and there . . . a few heroic "snipers." Where is that long list of invincible and challenging churches today? How many are now engaged in the same commitment of equipping saints for ministry by means of a strong Bible-teaching pulpit and a solid Sunday school balanced with an equally strong emphasis on application and discipleship?

Does that sound too severe, too negative? All right, let's take a simple four-question quiz:

1. How many influential churches can you name in America that are known for their biblical dynamic— places where you would be adequately fed and challenged, really "equipped"?
2. Among your friends who have moved out of your city to other areas of the country, how many are excited, healthy, and growing spiritually, thanks to a good church?
3. What continues to be the greatest need in evangelical seminaries among those planning to enter the pastorate?
4. How many young men can you list who are pursuing the pastoral ministry with enthusiasm, assurance, a heart for God, and a commitment to biblical exposition? Eighteen? Ten? Seven? Three?

It is not an exaggeration to say a famine is upon us—the worst kind of famine one can imagine. A famine Queen Victoria and her feasting peers knew nothing about.

But Amos did.

That ancient prophet had *us* in mind, not nineteenth-century Great Britain, when he recorded these poignant words:

"Behold, days are coming," declares the Lord GOD,
"When I will send a famine on the land,
Not a famine for bread or a thirst for water,
But rather for hearing the words of the LORD.
And people will stagger from sea to sea [coast to coast],
And from the north even to the east,
They will go to and fro to seek the word of the LORD,
But they will not find it" (Amos 8:11-12).

Read those words slowly. Read them aloud, American.

Read them and weep.

How firm a foundation, ye saints of the Lord,
Is laid for your faith in His excellent Word!
What more can He say than to you He hath said,
To you who for refuge to Jesus have fled?[14]

Ask yourself that question. As you pray, give God praise for His Word—inspired, reliable, penetrating, and eternal. Ask Him to keep you on your quest for character. If you are in a church where there is balance, a consistently strong, challenging pulpit, compassion, and zeal for the lost, regardless of the church's size, give Him your praise.

Read Psalm 119:97-106.

CHARACTER
IS NOT MADE
IN CRISIS—
IT IS ONLY
EXHIBITED.
—FREEMAN

running scared

It happened over forty years ago. The irony of it, however, amazes me to this day.

A mural artist named J. H. Zorthian read about a tiny boy who had been killed in traffic. His stomach churned as he thought of that ever happening to one of his three children. His worry became an inescapable anxiety. The more he imagined such a tragedy, the more fearful he became. His effectiveness as an artist was put on hold once he started running scared.

At last he surrendered to his obsession. Canceling his negotiations to purchase a large house in busy Pasadena, California, he began to seek a place where his children would be safe. His pursuit became so intense that he set aside all his work while scheming and planning every possible means to protect his children from harm. He tried to imagine the presence of danger in everything. The location of the residence was critical. It must be sizable and remote, so he bought twelve acres perched on a mountain at the end of a long, winding, narrow road. At each turn along the road he posted signs, "Children at Play." Before starting construction on the house itself, Zorthian personally built and fenced a play yard for his three children. He built it in such a way that it was impossible for a car to get within fifty feet of it.

Next . . . the house. With meticulous care he blended beauty and safety into the place. He put into it various shades of the designs he had concentrated in the murals he had hanging in forty-two public buildings in eastern cities. Only this time his objective was more than colorful art . . . most of all, it had to be safe and secure. He made sure of that. Finally, the garage was to be built. Only one automobile ever drove into that garage—Zorthian's.

He stood back and surveyed every possibility of danger to his children. He could think of only one remaining hazard. He had to back out of the garage. He might, in some hurried moment, back over one of the children. He immediately made plans for a protected turnaround. The contractor returned and set the forms for that additional area, but before the cement could be poured, a downpour stopped the project. It was the first rainfall in many weeks of a long West Coast drought.

If it had not rained that week, the concrete turnaround would have been completed and been in use by Sunday. That was February 9, 1947 . . . the day his eighteen-month old son, Tiran, squirmed away from his sister's grasp and ran behind the car as Zorthian drove it from the garage. *The child was killed instantly.*

There are no absolute guarantees. No fail-safe plans. No perfectly reliable designs. No completely risk-free arrangements. Life refuses to be that neat and clean. Not even the neurotics, who go to extreme measures to make positively sure, are protected from their obsessive fears. Those "best-laid plans of mice and men" continue to backfire, reminding us that living and risking go hand in hand. Running scared invariably blows up in one's face. All who fly risk crashing. All who drive risk colliding. All who run risk falling. All who walk risk stumbling. All who live risk *something*.

> To laugh is to risk appearing the fool.
> To weep is to risk appearing sentimental.
> To reach out for another is to risk involvement.
> To expose feelings is to risk exposing your
>   true self.
> To love is to risk not being loved in return.
> To hope is to risk despair.
> To try is to risk failure.

Want to know the shortest route to ineffectiveness? Start running scared. Try to cover every base at all times. Become paranoid over your front, your flanks, and your rear. Think about every possible peril, focus on the dangers, concern yourself with the "what ifs" instead of the "why nots?" Take no chances. Say no to courage and yes to caution. Expect the worst. Play your cards close to your vest. Let fear run wild. "To him who is in fear," said Sophocles, "everything rustles." Triple lock all doors. Keep yourself safely tucked away in the secure nest of inaction. And before you know it (to borrow from the late author, E. Stanley Jones), "the paralysis of analysis" will set in. So will loneliness, and finally isolation. No thanks!

How much better to take on a few ornery bears and lions, like David did. They ready us for giants like Goliath. How much more thrilling to step out into the Red Sea like Moses and watch God part the waters. Sure makes for exciting stuff to talk about while trudging around a miserable wilderness for the next forty years. How much more interesting to set sail for Jerusalem, like Paul, "not knowing what will happen to me there," than to spend one's days in monotonous Miletus, listening for footsteps and watching dull sunsets. Guard your heart from overprotection!

Happily, not all have opted for safety. Some have overcome, regardless of the risks. Some have merged into greatness despite adversity. They refuse to listen to their fears. Nothing anyone says or does holds them back. Disabilities and disappointments need not disqualify! As Ted Engstrom insightfully writes:

> Cripple him, and you have a Sir Walter Scott. Lock him in a prison cell, and you have a John Bunyan. Bury him in the snows of Valley Forge, and you have a George Washington. Raise him in abject poverty and you have an Abraham Lincoln. Strike him down with infantile paralysis, and he becomes Franklin Roosevelt. Burn him so severely that the doctors say he'll never walk again, and you have a Glenn Cunningham—who set the world's one-mile record in 1934. Deafen him and you have a Ludwig van Beethoven. Have him or her born black in a society filled with racial discrimination, and you have a Booker T. Washington, a Marian Anderson, a George Washington Carver. . . . Call him a slow learner, "retarded," and write him off as uneducable, and you have an Albert Einstein.[15]

Tell your fears where to get off; otherwise, your quest for character will be interrupted. Effectiveness—sometimes greatness—awaits those who refuse to run scared.

What comes from the Lord because it is impossible for humans to manufacture it? Wisdom. What comes from humans because it is impossible for the Lord to experience it? Worry. And what is it that brings wisdom and dispels worry? Worship. Let nothing detract from your time of personal worship today. Let nothing frighten you . . . nothing from yesterday's past, today's present, or tomorrow's future. Nothing.

Read 2 Timothy 1:3-14.

a downward spiral

Some of my most pleasurable memories take me back to a little bay off the gulf of Mexico. My maternal granddad owned a small cottage on that bay and was generous to share it with his extended brood. Throughout my adolescent years our family spent summer vacations down there: boating, swimming by the hour, jumping off piers, seining for shrimp, early-morning fishing, late-night floundering, but mainly *laughing* and *relaxing*.

While those years passed in family togetherness and fun, an ugly erosion was taking place. The waters of the bay were eating away at the bank of land between the cottage and the sea. Year after year, thanks to the rising and falling tide, a few hurricanes, and the normal lapping of waves at the shoreline, chunks of earth were being consumed by the bay. In all our busy activities and lazy hours of relaxation, no one ever talked about it or bothered to notice. In my childish innocence I never even thought about it. But I shall never forget the day all that changed. I did a little experiment late one summer day that made an indelible impression on my mind.

The previous year, our class in junior high school had studied erosion. The teacher did a good job of convincing us that even though we cannot see much happening or hear many warnings, erosion can occur right under our eyes. *Just because it's silent and slow doesn't mean it isn't devastating.* So, all alone the last day of our vacation that summer, I drove a big stake deep into the soil and then stepped off the distance between the stake and the sea—about fifteen feet, as I recall.

The next year we returned. Before sundown the first day we arrived, I returned to the stake and stepped off the distance; a little under twelve feet remained. The bay had gobbled up another three-plus feet—not in big gulps, understand, but an inch here and another inch or so there during the year that had passed. A downward spiral was underway. I've often wondered if I ever returned to that place of happy family memories, would the cottage still be standing, or would it have surrendered to the insatiable appetite of the sea?

A friend of mine who attended an elite college in the Midwest many years ago told me a similar story. There was this massive tree—sort of a treasured land-mark—where students had met for decades. No one could even imagine that campus without the giant oak that spread its limbs for all to enjoy. It seemed to be a perpetual part of the landscape . . . *until.* One day, with an enormous nerve-jolting C-R-A-C-K, the mighty giant gave up the ghost. Once down, all who grieved its passing could see what no one had bothered to notice. A downward spiral had continued for years. Month by month, season after season, an internal erosion was taking place. *Just because it was silent and slow didn't mean it wasn't dying.*

My interest is not simply with a cottage or a college . . . not nearly so much as with character. Ever so slightly, invisible moral and ethical germs can invade, bringing the beginning stages of a terminal disease. No one can tell by looking, for it happens imperceptibly. It's slower than a clock and far more silent. There are no chimes, not even a persistent ticking. An oversight here, a compromise there, a deliberate looking the other way, a softening, a yawn, a nod, a nap, a habit . . . a destiny. And before we know it, a chunk of character falls into the sea, a protective piece of bark drops onto the grass. What was once "no big thing" becomes, in fact, bigger than life itself. What started with inquisitive innocence terminates at destructive addiction.

The same downward spiral can impact a family. It's what I often refer to as the "domino effect." What is tolerated by mom and dad flows down to son and daughter. As Jeremiah once wept, ". . . the fathers have eaten sour grapes, and the children's teeth are set on edge" (Jeremiah 31:29). The tragedy is that it doesn't stop there. Those kids grow up, shaping a nation's future. Reminds me of a line out of John Steinbeck's letter to Adlai Stevenson:

There is a creeping all-pervading gas of immorality which starts in the nursery and does not stop until it reaches the highest offices, both corporate and governmental.[16]

Sociologist and historian Carle Zimmerman, in his 1947 book *Family and Civilization,* recorded his keen observations as he compared the disintegration of various cultures with the parallel decline of family life in those cultures. Eight specific patterns of domestic behavior typified the downward spiral of each culture Zimmerman studied.

- Marriage loses its sacredness . . . is frequently broken by divorce.
- Traditional meaning of the marriage ceremony is lost.
- Feminist movements abound.
- Increased public disrespect for parents and authority in general.
- Acceleration of juvenile delinquency, promiscuity, and rebellion.
- Refusal of people with traditional marriages to accept family responsibilities.
- Growing desire for and acceptance of adultery.
- Increasing interest in and spread of sexual perversions and sex-related crimes.[17]

That last one generally marks the final stage of societal disintegration. The "creeping, all-pervading gas" may be invisible, but, according to Zimmerman, it can be lethal.

Before closing today's reading with a shrug, spend sixty seconds scrutinizing your life. If you're married, step off a mental measurement of your marriage . . . your family. Think hard. Don't lie to yourself. Ask and answer a few tough questions. Compare "the way we were" with "the way we are." Look within the walls of your moral standard, your once-strong commitment to ethical excellence. Any termites in the timber? Don't be deceived by past years of innocence and fun. An ugly erosion may be taking place that you haven't bothered to notice. *Just because the changes are silent and slow doesn't mean things aren't deteriorating.*

As the pages of the calendar turn and turn again, we're reminded of the Lord's power to change the times and the seasons. Brisk blustery days replace hot, still ones. Flowers grace the fields and then fade away. Leaves bud on naked limbs, open wide to the summer breeze, then die in a flame of color. Take time today to delight in His presence as you acknowledge His right to bring change into your life. Are you sensitive to His working? Are you listening? Are you available and open to change? Tell Him today.

Read Ephesians 5:1-21.

rigidity

I have just put the phone down. I had no trouble finding myself in the story.

On the other end of the line was a pastor of a church of considerable size. He and I have been friends for about a decade. A sensitive, caring, tender man . . . maybe too tender, almost fragile at times. He's in an evangelical church that is strong and respected in the community. There is no reason he shouldn't be enjoying deeper feelings of fulfillment, greater power in the pulpit, and closer relationships with others. But he's not. Though he is seasoned in years, he is quickly losing heart. His words? "I want to quit." He's not a quitter, but today he's beginning to wonder if quitting might be best.

Why? Because he has run up against a thick wall of resistance. He has begun a creative program that breaks with the past, one that wouldn't ruffle many feathers in a place where innovation is welcomed and change is appreciated. But because a pocket of people in his flock is neither very innovative nor open, the man has encountered the wrath of Khan. I hurt for him, but there is very little I can do to help. I called because I had heard he was leaving (a false rumor) and I wanted to encourage him. Mainly, I felt he needed a listening ear and the reassurance that some-body, even though many miles away, still believed in him. I hope he felt affirmed.

I am praying that my friend won't toss in the towel, but I respect him too much to preach to him. There are numerous difficulties church leaders can and must withstand. Each may bring pain and disappointment, but because none strike at the core, hope helps us cope. We still have breathing room. Any leadership position has its occupational hazards, including minis-try. But there are a few tests that can be endured only so long. One of them is *rigidity*. I don't know of a better word for it. It's tough enough to deal with folks who choose to live that way themselves, but when they re-quire that of you, ultimately restricting the vision of a ministry, it becomes unbearable. Perhaps it is the closest anyone ever gets to feeling suffocated.

Why is rigidity so difficult for ministers to deal with? Why does it have such a tyrannical affect on churches? Three reasons come to mind.

First, because rigidity is seldom prompted by love. True love (the kind described in 1 Corinthians 13) ". . . is patient . . . kind . . . does not act unbecomingly; it does not seek its own" (vv. 4-5). In other words, love lets go of its own way. It releases. It is neither demand-ing nor possessive.

Second, because rigidity restrains creativity, thus blocking progress. Threatened by risk and the possibility of failure, it clips the future's wings—then later criticizes it for not flying.

Third, because rigidity is the trademark of legalism, the archenemy of any church on the move. Let legalism have enough rope and there will be a lynching of all new ideas, fresh thinking, and innovative programs. Yes, all. Freedom requires room to roam, space to stretch, leading to the excitement of exploration. Remove freedom and we wave enthusiasm a desperate, longing good-bye.

Pastor Eugene Peterson minces no words as he urges those who are free to be vigilant. Read this thoughtfully:

> There are people who do not want us to be free. They don't want us to be free before God, accepted just as we are by his grace. They don't want us to be free to express our faith originally and creatively in the world. They want to control us; they want to use us for their own purposes. They themselves refuse to live arduously and openly in faith, but huddle together with a few others and try to get a sense of approval by insisting that all look alike, talk alike and act alike, thus validating one another's worth. They try to enlarge their numbers only on the condition that new members act and talk and behave the way they do.
>
> These people infiltrate communities of faith "to spy out our freedom which we have in Christ Jesus" and not infrequently find ways to control, restrict, and reduce the lives of free Christians. Without being aware of it we become anxious about what others will say about us, obsessively concerned about what others

think we should do. We no longer live the good news but anxiously try to memorize and recite the script that someone else has assigned to us. In such an event we may be secure, but we will not be free. We may survive as a religious community, but we will not experience what it means to be human, alive in love and faith, expansive in hope.[18]

In the final analysis, rigidity puts dreams to death. Without dreams, life becomes dull, tedious, full of caution, inhibited. Instead of launching into new ventures, we hold back out of fear. Rigidity and risk cannot coexist.

On May 24, 1965, a thirteen-and-a-half-foot boat slipped quietly out of the marina at Falmouth, Massachusetts. Its destination? England. It would be the smallest craft ever to make the voyage. Its name? *Tinkerbelle*. Its pilot? Robert Manry, a copyeditor for the *Cleveland Plain Dealer*, who felt that ten years at the desk was enough boredom for a while. So he took a leave of absence to fulfill his secret dream.

Manry was afraid . . . not of the ocean, but of all those people who would try to talk him out of the trip. So he didn't share it with many, just some relatives, and especially his wife Virginia, his greatest source of support.

The trip? Anything but pleasant. He spent harrowing nights of sleeplessness trying to cross shipping lanes without getting run down and sunk. Weeks at sea caused his food to become tasteless. Loneliness, that age-old monster of the deep, led to terrifying hallucinations. His rudder broke three times. Storms swept him overboard, and had it not been for the rope he had knotted around his waist, he would never have been able to pull himself back on board. Finally, after seventy-eight days alone at sea, he sailed into Falmouth, England.

During those nights at the tiller, he had fantasized about what he would do once he arrived. He expected simply to check into a hotel, eat dinner alone, then the next morning see if, perhaps, the Associated Press might be interested in his story. Was he in for a surprise! Word of his approach had spread far and wide. To his amazement, three hundred vessels, with horns blasting, escorted *Tinkerbelle* into port. And forty thousand people stood screaming and cheering him to shore.

Robert Manry, the copyeditor turned dreamer, became an overnight hero. His story has been told around the world. But Robert couldn't have done it alone. Standing on the dock was an even greater hero—Virginia. Refusing to be rigid and closed back when Robert's dream was taking shape, she encouraged him on . . . willing to risk . . . allowing him the freedom to pursue his dream.

Pacesetting ministries cannot become that without dreamers who weary of only "maintenance" year in, year out. The quest for character is accelerated in a context of freedom, encouragement, and risk. We need more Roberts who have the creativity and the tenacity to break with boredom and try the unusual. But even more, we need the Virginias who won't allow rigidity to rule the roost.

Tell me, do you have any trouble finding yourself in that story?

Vision. It is essential for survival. It is spawned by faith, sustained by hope, sparked by imagination and strengthened by enthusiasm. It is greater than sight, deeper than a dream, broader than an idea. Vision encompasses vast vistas outside the realm of the predictable, the safe, the expected. No wonder we perish without it! Ask God to stretch your vision today . . . to encourage you with visionary plans as you walk in His presence.

Read Hebrews 11.

curiosity

"Curious George" is a monkey. He's the main character in a series of children's books which my oldest son used to love as a lad. We sat by the hours during his childhood and laughed like crazy at the outlandish predicaments little George experienced simply because his curiosity got the best of him.

The stories always followed the same basic pattern. George would casually drift into a new area, his inquisitive nature prompting him to investigate. The first step was neither wrong nor harmful, just a bit questionable. Invariably, George would not be satisfied with his initial encounter and discoveries, but would probe deeper . . . peer longer . . . pry further . . . until the novelty of the situation took on a new dimension, the dimension of *danger*.

Ultimately, nothing short of tragedy occurred— and the one who suffered the most was our dear little long-tailed friend, a curious primate named George.

Curiosity—at one point the sign of a healthy, sometimes ingenious mind . . . the spark that drives hungry seekers into the labyrinth of truth, refusing to stop short of thorough examination.

Curiosity—that time-worn gate hinged by determination and discipline that leads to the ecstasy of discovery through the agony of pursuit.

Curiosity—the built-in teacher that instantly challenges the status quo . . . that turns a wayward waif into a Churchill, a hopeless mute into a Keller, and a Missouri farm boy into a Disney.

Curiosity—the quality most often squelched in children by thoughtless, hurried adults who view questions as "interruptions" rather than the driving desire to lift one's mental wheels beyond the weary rut of the known.

But what a deceitful role it can play!

Remove the safety belt of biblical parameters and curiosity will send our vehicle of learning on a collision course, destined for disaster. It has a way of making us meddle in others' affairs, for curiosity is by nature intrusive. It dresses wrong in the most attractive apparel known to man. It hides the damnable consequences of adultery behind the alluring attire of excitement, soft music, and a warm embrace. It masquerades the heartaches of drug abuse and alcoholism by dressing them in the Levis and sweater of a handsome, adventurous sailboat skipper.

Curiosity is the single, most needed commodity depended upon to keep the world of the occult busy and effective. It alone is sufficient reason for the box-office triumphs of movies that major on sadistic violence or demonic encounters. Remove curiosity from the heart and *The Exorcist* is a sick joke . . . and even the Church of Satan is laughed to scorn.

But it *cannot be removed!* Curiosity is as much a part of your human nature as your elbow is a part of your arm. Your enemy knows that fact, and counts on it. He started with Eve . . . and he continues with thee. He's a master at the black art of subterfuge, a two-bit word for setting a trap that makes your curiosity sit up, lean forward, and move in. Remember, he's been setting traps a lot longer than you and I have been dodging them. If he can garnish the hook with the right bait—designed to arouse just enough curiosity— it's *only a matter of time*.

James sees it clearly and says it straight:

> Let no one say when he is tempted, "I am being tempted by God"; for God cannot be tempted by evil, and He Himself does not tempt anyone. But each one is tempted when he is carried away and enticed by his own lust. Then when lust has conceived, it gives birth to sin; and when sin is accomplished, it brings forth death (James 1:13-15).

Of course, we need not be the victims of our foolish curiosity. Powerful help is available to guide us through Satan's maze of mirages, booby traps and landmines. Our Savior has already walked the course we're walking now—and knows how to guide us through unscathed.

By walking at His side, you can get the monkey off your back . . . only this time its name isn't George.

The Spirit versus the flesh. We've all witnessed the battle. We've all experienced the difference! With the flesh in control there is comparison and struggle, agitation, irritation, force, and offense. With the Spirit, however, there is release and relief . . . deep satisfaction, joy that lasts, love that isn't fickle, peace that isn't fleeting. Worship Him today in truth *and* in the Spirit.

Read Galatians 5:16-26.

parental negligence

How's it going with you and the kids?

That question may not apply to you, but I have a hunch that *many* of my readers are still in the process of training and rearing. So, for your sake . . . *how's it going*? What word(s) would you check to describe your overall relationship with your offspring?

—Challenging	—Impossible	—Adventurous
—Exciting	—Strained	—Heartbreaking
—Angry	—Fun	—Pleasant
—Threatening	—Impatient	—Busy

If you want to get your eyes open to the real facts, ask your kids at the supper table this evening. Ask *them* to describe their feelings about you and the home. But I'd better warn you—it may hurt! However, it could be the first step back in the right direction toward harmony and genuine love being restored under your roof. Fact is, you may be pleasantly surprised. Parents are often more critical of themselves than necessary.

Needless to say, having a Christian home is no guarantee against disharmony. The old nature can still flare up. The gnarled roots of self-centered habits can tangle communication lines. Helpful biblical principles can be ignored. Face the truth, my friend. Stop right now and *think about your home*. Why not bite off a chunk of time during the next few months for a single purpose—to evaluate the present condition of your home and then to set in motion the necessary steps needed to strengthen the weaknesses you uncover. Now, an evaluation is no good if all it leads to is guilt and hurt. To stop there would be like a surgeon stopping the operation immediately after making his incision. All it would leave is continued problems, a lot of pain, and a nasty scar.

Let me urge you to use this period of time as an opportunity to get next to your children . . . to come to grips with the barriers that are blocking the flow of your love and affection (and theirs) . . . to evaluate how much character development is going on . . . to *face the facts* before the nagging sore spots lead to a permanent, domestic disease. Guard your heart from negligence! Three biblical cases come to my mind, which should relieve you a little as you realize you're not alone in this struggle.

1. *Rebekah*—who favored Jacob over Esau . . . and used him to deceive his father, Isaac, which led to a severe family breakdown (Genesis 27).
2. *Eli*—who was judged by God because of his lack of discipline and failure to stand firm when his boys began to run wild (1 Samuel 3:11-14).
3. *David*—who committed the same sin against his son, Adonijah, by never restraining him or crossing him throughout his early training (1 Kings 1:5-6).

You see, no one is immune . . . not even Bible characters. Not even *you*. So then, move ahead! Refuse to pamper your parental negligence any longer. If this brief chapter spurs you on, it will have accomplished its purpose.

As I hang my close on this first section, let me do so by quoting an excerpt from an article published years ago by the United States Chamber of Commerce. It is a list of twelve rules on:

How to Train Your Child to be a Delinquent

1. When your kid is still an infant, give him everything he wants. This way he'll think the world owes him a living when he grows up.
2. When he picks up swearing and off-color jokes, laugh at him, encourage him. As he grows up, he'll pick up "cuter" phrases that will floor you.
3. Never give him any spiritual training. Wait until he is twenty-one and let him decide for himself.
4. Avoid using the word *wrong*. It will give your child a guilt complex. You can condition him to believe later, when he is arrested for stealing a car, that society is against him and he is being persecuted.
5. Pick up after him—his books, shoes, and clothes. Do everything for him so he will be experienced in throwing all responsibility onto others.
6. Let him read all printed matter he can get his hands on . . . [never think of monitoring his TV programs]. Sterilize the silverware, but let him feast his mind on garbage.
7. Quarrel frequently in his presence. Then he won't be too surprised when his home is broken up later.

8. Satisfy his every craving for food, drink, and comfort. Every sensual desire must be gratified; denial may lead to harmful frustrations.
9. Give your child all the spending money he wants. Don't make him earn his own. Why should he have things as tough as you did?
10. Take his side against neighbors, teachers, and policemen. They're all against him.
11. When he gets into real trouble, make up excuses for yourself by saying, "I never could do anything with him; he's just a bad seed."
12. Prepare for a life of grief.

Okay, okay . . . so maybe that's a little too sarcastic. But before tossing out the baby with the bathwater, better take a closer look. How *is* it going with you and the kids?

TODAY'S Quest

Home is indeed where life makes up its mind. It is there—with fellow family members—we hammer out our convictions on the anvil of relationships. It is there we cultivate the valuable things in life, like attitudes, memories, beliefs, and most of all, character. Give God thanks today for His help in using your home to develop these all-important essentials. Praise Him also for a "home" among His people, for that great family of families known as His Church.

Read Deuteronomy 6:1-9.

beauty...at a distance

This is L.A.?

Fresh-fallen snow has blanketed the range of mountains on the northeast rim of the Los Angeles basin. I caught my first glimpse driving to the office this February morning. You'd think we were on the edge of the Alps! As I came up over a hill I found myself smiling and saying aloud, "Beautiful!"

Usually the smog blocks that view, but last night's rain washed the skies crystal clear, giving us a rare day to enjoy the whitecapped range, with snow now down to the 2,000-foot level. Seventy-five miles away, the mountains *are* beautiful.

Yesterday was different however; different as night and day. Early in the morning Cynthia and I decided to enjoy a few hours together up near Lake Arrowhead, a quiet hamlet nestled in a crevice of those mountains at about 6,000 feet. The clouds looked a little threatening before we left, but nothing to worry about. A brisk walk a mile high would be refreshing and invigorating . . . and long overdue. So we got bundled up and took off. What we encountered could easily make one of those you'll-never-believe-it *Reader's Digest* articles, but

I'll not bother to submit it. I will tell you a little, since the whole nightmare carries with it some tremendous lessons.

About the time we reached 4,500 feet, narrow Highway 18 began to gather white dust. The temperature was right at freezing, the clouds were thick, and the wind had picked up considerably. I could have turned back then—and should have—but we were only fifteen or so minutes from our destination. We pressed on. The "freak storm," as some in the village called it, was surprising to those at Arrowhead and, I must admit, frightening to us. It became increasingly more obvious that things weren't going to get better, so we decided to cut our visit short. By now, the wind was howling and the snow was swirling. Disappointed, we piled back into the car and began a journey that we shall never forget if we share *another* thirty-two years together as man and wife. A brief conversation haunted me for the next several miles. It had occurred before we left:

"Shouldn't we buy tire chains?" she asked.

"Naw, this won't be any problem," he answered.

"Are you sure? We're downhill all the way back," she reminded.

"Don't worry, hon. We'll be outa this in no time," he lied.

An hour and a half (which seemed more like an unbelievable decade) later we reached San Bernardino.

Between 6,000 feet and sea level, only the Lord and we know what occurred for sure. I have driven since I was fourteen. I have been in just about every conceivable situation—alone or with a car full of kids, in desert or mountain, the dead of night or blistering sun, sports car or thirty-two-foot motorhome, across town or across the continent, in fog or downpour or sleet—but *never* have I spent a more hair-raising ninety minutes in my life. There was no sin—mortal or venial, thought, word, or deed—I didn't confess. No prayer I didn't use. No verse I didn't claim. You know how folks say that when you're drowning, all your life passes before your eyes? I can assure you the same is true as you fishtail your way down a glazed, winding, single-lane mountain highway, trying every maneuver known to man just to keep from colliding with an oncoming car or crashing into the mountainside . . . or toppling over the precipice.

Tony Bennett may have left his heart in San Francisco, but we left our stomach, kidney, liver, and bladder all the way down treacherous Highway 18. My steering wheel has new grip marks that were not there two days ago. And if anyone has the gall to ask me if I plan to purchase tire chains, I need to warn you ahead of time, I'll punch you in the mouth. Trust me, this stubborn guy learned his lesson . . . permanently. Everyone with Swindoll blood will own snow chains. I'm even going to see if they make chains for bikes and trikes!

There's another lesson, one I will think of every time I see any beautiful snowcapped mountain range.

It may seem beautiful from a distance, but when you get real close there is a different scene entirely. Behind that beauty are bitter cold, screaming winds, blinding snow, icy roads, raw fear, and indescribable dangers. Distance feeds our fantasy. Any mountain range seems more beautiful when viewed from a sunlit street seventy-five miles away. Small wonder artists paint those high-priced scenes of breathtaking grandeur . . . most of them do so in warm, safe studios in the city! Put them in the back seat of a four-wheel vehicle where everything is a blur and survival is one's only goal, and I guarantee you, the canvas will look different.

There's another more personal lesson. From a distance we're all beautiful people. Well-dressed, nice smile, friendly looking, cultured, under control, at peace. But what a different picture when someone comes up close and gets in touch! What appeared so placid is really a mixture: winding roads of insecurity and uncertainty, maddening gusts of lust, greed, self-indulgence, pathways of pride glazed over with a slick layer of hypocrisy; all this shrouded in a cloud of fear of being found out. From a distance we dazzle . . . up close we're tarnished. Put enough of us together and we may resemble an impressive mountain range. But when you get down into the shadowy crevices . . . the Alps we ain't.

I'm convinced that's why our Lord means so much to us. He scrutinizes our path. He is intimately acquainted with all our ways. Darkness and light are alike to Him. Not one of us is hidden from His sight. All things are open and laid bare before Him: our darkest secret, our deepest shame, our stormy past, our worst thought, our hidden motive, our vilest imagination . . . even our vain attempts to cover the ugly with snow-white beauty. He comes up close. He sees it all. He knows our frame. He remembers we are dust. Best of all, He loves us still.

TODAY'S Quest

It's awesome to realize today was in God's mind and plan long before this earth was created. He knew you would be where you are at this very moment, living in your present circumstances, facing the kind of pressures you're enduring . . . and experiencing this moment of quiet reflection. Bow and thank Him. Turn over the controls of your life to Him. Admit your weakness, your hypocrisy, your tendency to worry, your deep need of His presence and counsel in your life. Take a few minutes right now to become completely preoccupied with Him . . . who has lovingly brought you to your knees.

Read Psalm 32.

CHARACTER IS SIMPLY
LONG HABIT CONTINUED.
—*PLUTARCH*

Part 2

GIVE YOUR HEART

We have all seen people who live defensive lives. They've got that look about them . . . always watching their flank, forever on guard, cautious. Somehow they feel the need to hold back, lest they get ripped off. Even well-meaning folks can overlearn the value of being on the alert. The telltale sign is the development of a watch-dog mentality that lacks the vulnerability of openness and the risks of love.

To balance out your character you need to do more than *guard* your heart. It is the flip side that makes you authentic . . . you also need to *give* your heart. To resist releasing yourself for fear of getting burned may seem safe, but in the long run it is lethal.

No one ever said it better than C. S. Lewis:

To love at all is to be vulnerable. Love anything, and your heart will certainly be wrung and possibly be broken. If you want to make sure of keeping it intact, you must give your heart to no one, not even to an animal. Wrap it carefully round with hobbies and little luxuries; avoid all entanglements; lock it up safe in the casket or coffin of your selfishness. But in that casket—safe, dark, motionless, airless—it will change. It will not be broken; it will become unbreakable,

impenetrable, irredeemable. . . . The only place outside Heaven where you can be perfectly safe from all
the dangers . . . of love is Hell.[19]

There is so much more to life than being safe.
The Bible is full of exhortations and illustrations point-
ing to the importance of letting ourselves go, being
who we are, giving what we can.

The quest for character calls for big chunks of our
life to be given away. In fact, Scripture promises that
we shall be rewarded in the same measure we give
ourselves to others.

A heart kept permanently closed keeps people at
a distance. A heart that risks being open invites them
in, has nothing to hide, promotes generosity, prompts
vulnerability, demonstrates love. If you wish to leave
this earth a better place than you found it, bringing
out the best in others, you'll want to give your heart.

The pages that follow will encourage you to do
that.

giving with gusto

"When the heart is right the feet are swift."

That's the way Thomas Jefferson put it many years ago. There are other ways to say the same thing: A happy spirit takes the grind out of giving. A positive attitude makes sacrifice a pleasure. When the morale is high the motivation is strong. When there is joy down inside, no challenge seems too great. The grease of gusto frees the gears of generosity.

And have you noticed how contagious such a spirit becomes? Not only do we feel the wind at our backs, others do as well. And when we are surrounded by that dynamic, a fresh surge of determination sweeps over us. You cannot stop it!

A close friend recently gave me a small paperback entitled *Great War Speeches* . . . a compilation of the most stirring speeches by Sir Winston Churchill. I had already read most of them, but in rereading them over the past several days I found myself once again stimulated . . . prodded to do better, to reach higher, to give greater measures of myself. Describing courageous warriors, he wrote:

> Every morn brought forth a noble change
> And every change brought forth a noble knight.[20]

115

Reminds me of David's words after Araunah offered the king one of his possessions for nothing. "No, but I will surely buy it from you for a price, for I will not offer burnt offerings to the LORD my God which cost me nothing" (2 Samuel 24:24). David refused a handout.

I love the application the late great preacher John Henry Jowett drew from David's words: "*Ministry that costs nothing, accomplishes nothing.*" For too long God's people have drifted along passively dreaming for things to change. It's time to act. It's time to make things change. And while we're at it, I suggest we have the time of our lives. Let's do so with gusto!

Can you recall the statement Paul makes in the second letter to the Corinthians? It is perhaps the foundational reference in Scripture linking joy with giving. "Let each one do just as he has purposed in his heart; not grudgingly [the word means "reluctantly"] or under compulsion ["feeling forced because of what others may say or think"]; for God loves a cheerful giver" (2 Corinthians 9:7). The term *cheerful*, remember, comes from a Greek word, *hilaros*, from which we get our word *hilarious*. And it's placed first in the original statement. Literally, "for the *hilarious* giver God prizes." Why? Because hilarious givers have swift feet. They give with gusto!

- When the Israelites gave themselves and their belongings to construct the tabernacle in the wilderness, their gusto was so evident they had to be told not to give anymore (Exodus 36:6-7).

- When the people in Jerusalem rallied around Nehemiah and rebuilt that wall, their gusto resulted in a record-breaking achievement (Nehemiah 2:17-18, 4:6, 6:15-16).
- When Jesus challenged His followers to be unselfish, He taught that it is "more blessed to give than to receive," connecting joy with our financial investments in eternal things (Acts 20:35).

Want to bring back the gusto? Want to become a "noble knight" at the round table of generosity? Let me remind you of four simple suggestions. They work for me.

1. *Reflect on God's gifts to you.* Hasn't He been good? Better than we deserve. Good health. Happy family. Sufficient food, clothing, and shelter. Close friends . . . and so much more.

2. *Remind yourself of His promises regarding generosity.* Call to mind a few biblical principles that promise the benefits of sowing bountifully. Bumper crops, don't forget, are God's specialty.

3. *Examine your heart.* Nobody but you can do this. Open that private vault and ask several hard questions, like:

   - Is my giving proportionate to my income?
   - Am I motivated by guilt . . . or by contagious joy?
   - If someone else knew the level of my giving to God's work, would I be a model to follow?
   - Have I prayed about giving . . . or am I just an impulsive responder?

4. *Trust God to honor consistent generosity.* Here's the big step, but it's essential. Go for it! When you really believe God is leading you to make a significant contribution—release your restraint and develop the habit of generosity. I seriously doubt that generosity has ever hurt many people!

As the people of God, we have enormous financial challenges before us, don't we? But magnificent goals are achievable if . . . *if* our spirits stay happy . . . *if* our morale stays high. The quest for character includes generosity! Let's make this year our all-time best. Let's give to the work of our Lord as we have never ever given before. With great gusto. With contagious joy. With outstanding offerings of a sacrificial nature, like noble knights of old.

If our hearts are right, our feet will be swift.

Forbid it Lord, that our roots become too firmly attached to this earth, that we should fall in love with things.

Help us to understand that the pilgrimage of this life is but an introduction, a preface, a training school for what is to come.

Then shall we see all of life in its true perspective. Then shall we not fall in love with the things of time, but come to love the things that endure. Then shall we be saved from the tyranny of possessions which we have no leisure to enjoy, of prosperity whose care becomes a burden. Give us, we pray, the courage to simplify our lives.[21]

—Peter Marshall

Read Exodus 35:3-9; 20-29; 36:2-7.

two memorable minutes

Depth, not length, is important. Not how long you take to talk but how much you say. Not how flowery and eloquent you sound but how sincerely and succinctly you speak . . . that's what is important . . . that's what is remembered. Two memorable minutes can be more effective than two marathon hours.

Step into the time tunnel and travel back with me to a field in Pennsylvania. The year is 1863. The month is July. The place is Gettysburg. Today it is a series of quiet rolling hills full of markings and memories. But back then it was a battleground . . . more horrible than we can imagine.

During the first days of that month, 51,000 were killed, wounded, or missing in what would prove the decisive Union victory of the Civil War. Anguished cries of the maimed and dying made a wailing chorus as the patients were hurried to improvised operating tables. One nurse recorded these words in her journal: "For seven days the tables literally ran with blood." Wagons and carts were filled to overflowing with amputated arms and legs, wheeled off to a deep trench, dumped, and buried. Preachers quoted the Twenty-third Psalm over and over as fast as their lips could say it while brave soldiers breathed their last.

The aftermath of any battlefield is always grim, but this was one of the worst. A national cemetery was proposed. A consecration service was planned. The date was set: November 19. The commission invited none other than the silver-tongued Edward Everett to deliver the dedication speech. Known for his cultured words, patriotic fervor, and public appeal, the orator, a former congressman and governor of Massachusetts, was a natural for the historic occasion. Predictably, he accepted.

In October President Lincoln announced his intentions to attend the ceremonies. This startled the commissioners, who had not expected Mr. Lincoln to leave the Capitol in wartime. Now, how could he not be asked to speak? They were nervous, realizing how much better an orator Everett was than Lincoln. Out of courtesy, they wrote the President on November 2, asking him to deliver "a few appropriate remarks." Certainly Lincoln knew the invitation was an afterthought, but it mattered little. When the battle of Gettysburg had begun, he had dropped to his knees and pleaded with God not to let the nation perish. He felt his prayer had been answered. His sole interest was to sum up what he passionately felt about his beloved country.

With such little time for preparation before the day of dedication, Lincoln worried over his words. He confided to a friend that his talk was not going smoothly. Finally, he forced himself to be satisfied with his "ill-prepared speech." He arrived at Gettysburg the day before the ceremonies in time to attend a large dinner that evening. With Edward Everett across the room, surrounded by numerous admirers, the President must have felt all the more uneasy. He excused himself from the after-dinner activities to return to his room and work a bit more on his remarks.

At midnight a telegram arrived from his wife: "The doctor has just left. We hope dear Taddie is slightly better." Their ten-year-old son Tad had become seriously ill the day before. Since the President and his wife had already lost two of their four children, Mrs. Lincoln had insisted that he not leave. But he had felt he must. With a troubled heart, he extinguished the lights in his room and struggled with sleep.

About nine o'clock the next morning, Lincoln copied his address onto two small pages and tucked them into his coat pocket . . . put on his stovepipe hat, tugged white gloves over his hands, and joined the procession of dignitaries. He could hardly bear the sight as they passed the blood-soaked fields where scraps of men's lives littered the area . . . a dented canteen, a torn picture of a child, a boot, a broken rifle. Mr. Lincoln was seized by grief. Tears ran down into his beard.

Shortly after the chaplain of the Senate gave the invocation, Everett was introduced. At sixty-nine, the grand old gentleman was slightly afraid he might forget his long, memorized speech, but once he got into it, everything flowed. His words rang smoothly across the field like silver bells. He knew his craft. Voice fluctuation. Tone. Dramatic gestures. Eloquent pauses. Lincoln stared in fascination. Finally, one hour and fifty-seven minutes later, the orator took his seat as the crowd roared its enthusiastic approval.

At two o'clock in the afternoon, Lincoln was introduced. As he stood to his feet, he turned nervously to Secretary Seward and muttered, "They won't like it." Slipping on his steel spectacles, he held the two pages in his right hand and grabbed his lapel with his left. He never moved his feet or made any gesture with his hands. His voice, high-pitched, almost squeaky, carried over the crowd like a brass bugle. He was serious and sad at the beginning . . . but a few sentences into the speech, his face and voice came alive. As he spoke, "The world will little note nor long remember . . . ," he almost broke, but then he caught himself and was strong and clear. People listened on tiptoe.

Suddenly, he was finished.

No more than two minutes after he had begun he stopped. His talk had been so prayerlike it seemed almost inappropriate to applaud. As Lincoln sank into his settee, John Young of the *Philadelphia Press* whispered, "Is that all?" The President answered, "Yes, that's all."

Over one hundred twenty years have passed since that historic event. Can anyone recall *one line* from Everett's two-hour Gettysburg address? Depth, remember, not length, is important. Lincoln's two minutes have become among the most memorable two minutes in the history of our nation.

Some of you reading these words have felt an inner nudge to spend more time talking to your heavenly Father this year. Even as you've considered that need, however, you've convinced yourself that "you just don't have time." After all, you're not a spiritual giant, and what could possibly be accomplished in the ten-, five-, or *two-minute* blocks of time you have to spare?

It might surprise you. With God, the possibilities are limitless. Recently, I heard of a youth leader who mistakenly arrived at a college campus classroom half an hour before he was scheduled to speak. Hating to waste time, he found himself fidgeting. What in the world was he going to do with himself for thirty minutes? *Well*, he thought, *I guess I could pray.* He did. And the vision God gave him for America's youth during that half hour burns undiminished in his soul to this day. His ministry touches tens of thousands of teens every year.

History won't let us forget the day when one man accomplished more in two minutes than another did in two hours. How much more should we not underestimate the power of "two" minutes with God.

So what if you find yourself with only minutes to spare? Invest them in conversation with your great God. Give your heart in full devotion! Time is like character; it's depth that counts in the long run.

John R. W. Stott once admitted the truth that many of us have felt but failed to confess: "The thing I know will give me the deepest joy—namely, to be alone and unhurried in the presence of God, aware of His presence, my heart open to worship Him—is often the thing I least want to do." Today our living Lord welcomes you into His presence. Even though you may admit to some reluctance, God nevertheless awaits those few precious moments when you lift your face and heart to Him.

Read Psalm 100; Hebrews 10:19-25.

underdogs

It was a contrast of incredible proportions. I'm referring to back-to-back scenes in which my wife, Cynthia, and I found ourselves last Saturday night . . . from the sublime to the ridiculous. Literally.

Scene 1: Elegant, dignified, formal, gracious, artful, quiet, lovely. Our church's chancel pipe organ played to perfection by two of the best to an audience of music lovers who appreciated the finer things and understood the technical things. Like "four-manual console" and "quadruple-memory system" and the difference between a "rank" and a "stop" . . . a "general piston" and a "crescendo pedal." We're talking a classy cross-section of gifted artists and musical connoisseurs.

Scene 2: Loud, boisterous, rough, sittin' on the floor in our grubbies, eatin' finger-licken' chicken from the Colonel's . . . watchin' a fight on TV between a runt named Spinks and a grunt named Holmes at our older son's place. The room was packed with a whole different group—not one of whom seemed that concerned about a balanced solo expression pedal. As I recall, nobody even asked us about the eight-foot Vox Humana pipe or the swell-to-great sixteen-inch coupler. The conversation was reduced to a five-inch longer reach and a twenty-plus pound weight advantage. And instead of quiet applause there were explosions of earsplitting screams.

You've heard of some who would rather "fight than switch." Well, we had to switch for the fight. Even brought along our jeans. Somehow a three-piece suit and a greasy drumstick didn't mix.

It was wild!

As I sat there between the coffee table and the sofa with our granddaughter Chelsea on my lap and a chicken thigh in my hand, I found myself thoroughly enjoying the contrast. Suddenly, I was intrigued by the fact that people in family rooms, recreation rooms, bars, and cars all over the country were yelling and screaming for a couple of guys they didn't even know. And chances were good that most of us were pulling for the same scrappy kid who had the audacity to get into the ring with that massive brute whose record stood at 48 and 0. Neither one of those boxers could've cared less about harmonic flute pipes or six-toe pistons or bombarde swell pedals. They had only one simple objective that hot Saturday night—to win. And everybody with any sense said it would be the champ, not the challenger.

That's what the majority always says.

- Wellington doesn't stand a chance against Napoleon.
- Baylor over USC? The Eagles over the Redskins? Don't make me laugh!

- Great Britain will never withstand Hitler's Luftwaffe.
- America's hockey team cannot possibly whip the Soviets.
- A rag-tag bunch of revolutionaries bringing England to her knees?
- "Chariots of Fire" winning the Oscar?
- A self-educated, Bible-quoting, Kentucky "hill-billy" becoming President of the United States?
- A no-name nun in Calcutta awarded the Nobel?

Shades of the Valley of Elah! Frightened Israel *versus* brutal Philistia. Jimmy the Greek would've laughed. Hands down, Goliath gets the nod. Place your bets on a sure thing, folks. That little Bethlehemite scampering up the slope must have looked like a tick on a grizzly's belly. A bee buzzing a behemoth. Who would have ever guessed the outcome? But who hasn't applauded it down inside?

We love it when the underdog gets the prize. Deep within us is a private chamber where loud celebration breaks out when the odds bite the dust. When the student stumps the scholar. When the pickup beats the Porsche. When the debate team from a struggling little school whips a group of snooty Ivy League hot-shots. When a smiling challenger with a twinkle in his eye outfoxes and outboxes a scowling champion who had become, in sportswriter Jim Murray's words, "a fistfighter locked in a cage of his own sour hostility." By the tightest of margins, Spinks pulled it off—and our place came unglued. Peanuts, chicken bones, chips and dip went airborne. Everybody jumped and jived and yelled and laughed . . . *except* Chelsea. She cried. She didn't understand.

Someday she will.

As she grows older, and true character emerges in her life, she will learn society's unwritten laws, which include such things as "poetic justice" and "turnabout is fair play." And she will begin to see Solomon's words come to pass:

> *the swiftest person does not always win the race;*
> *nor the strongest man the battle, . . . wise men are*
> *often poor, skillful men are not necessarily famous*
> . . . (Ecclesiastes 9:11, TLB).

Someday, little Chelsea will learn about the ultimate underdog. She will discover that born into the worst of settings was a tiny baby boy named Jesus, who came to save people from their sins. A contrast of incredible proportions—in a lowly manger, the long-awaited Messiah! And she will smile as she believes in Him. She may even laugh as she tells her granddaddy about it. Down deep in my "chamber," I will celebrate. I may even hear great swells of pipe organ music.

And as she sits on my lap and laughs, I will cry.

TODAY'S Quest

"... I have learned to be content in whatever circumstances I am," wrote the great apostle Paul (Philippians 4:11). Today, you may find yourself in difficult straits. You may be churning like the sea with worry and fretful uneasiness. Take time to read Philippians 4, noting especially verses 6-7. Read those verses a second time, more slowly. As you seek your Lord this day, give Him your anxiety. Ask for His peace, the same contentment "in whatever circumstance" Paul had.

intercession

I know, I know. You've heard people speak on this subject before. Maybe even last Sunday. You heard . . . but did you really listen? *Hearing* is the ability to discriminate sound vibrations transmitted to the brain. *Listening* is making sense of what is heard. Honestly now, did those words on prayer make sense to you?

And on top of all that is the loss-of-memory factor. Did you know that *immediately* after most people hear someone speak, only half of what was heard is remembered? Within two weeks, only one-fourth is retained—and some of that is fuzzy.

Toward the end of 2 Thessalonians 1, Paul admits, "We pray for you always. . . ." When we pray for someone, we *intercede*. That means we mentally get involved in their world as we deliberately make contact with God on their behalf. This, admittedly, is only one aspect of prayer, but it's a mighty important one!

Honestly now . . . are you involved in this activity about which you've heard so many sermons? Do you know where to begin?

Let's start with a list . . . actual names of people, and in parentheses you might write at least one need you are aware of. Put both on the left side of a three-by-five card or a half sheet of paper. On the right side, leave room for answers. You may want to add the date God answered your request. For example:

Name/Need	Answer	Date
Barbara (surgery)	Successful/but still in pain	3/10
Phil (school test)	Did well!	3/17
Mom and Dad (move?)	Still uncertain	
Jim and Jill (couples' retreat)	Communication improved	3/14-16
Sandi (job interview next Monday)		

Each Sunday afternoon is a good time to reflect on and update the card. You may need a new one. Maybe a phone call would be necessary to find out how God is working. Keep the list handy and while you're waiting for an appointment or driving to the store or to pick up the kids, review . . . get involved . . . intercede! Trust me, this will provide a whole new dimension to your walk with Christ. It will definitely get you out of your own personal world.

While reading through a section of 1 Samuel this week, I ran across a passage of Scripture that illustrates so graphically the value—the essential importance—of our praying for others.

Samuel is in the thick of it. His nation is going through a tough, uncertain transitional period. They have pressed for a king and gotten their way. It fell Samuel's lot to confront them . . . to spell out the lack of wisdom in their stubborn urgency to be "like all the other nations." They saw the foolishness in their decision *after* the fact (isn't that usually the way it is?). On top of their guilt, they witnessed the Lord's sending thunder and rain that same day, which only intensified their fears.

What next? Could they go on, having blown it so royally? Wisely, they made the right request of Samuel:

> *Pray for your servants . . . for we have added to all our sins this evil by asking for ourselves a king* (1 Samuel 12:19).

Greathearted Samuel must have smiled as he reassured them.

> *. . . far be it from me that I should sin against the Lord by ceasing to pray for you . . ."* (v. 23).

He had already been praying for them, so he promised not to stop. To do so would be a "sin against the Lord." Those on a quest for character call that important.

There is no more significant involvement in another's life than prevailing, consistent prayer. It is more helpful than a gift of money, more encouraging than a strong sermon, more effective than a compliment, more reassuring than a physical embrace.

Far be it from us that we should sin against the Lord by ceasing to pray for one another. I know, I know. You've heard about prayer all your life. You've even been encouraged to give your heart to faithful intercession. But the question is: Are you *doing* it?

"I love the Lord, because He hears my voice and my supplications. Because He has inclined His ear to me, therefore I shall call upon Him as long as I live" (Psalm 116:1-2). The psalmist declares that his love for God is prompted by His willingness to listen when he prays . . . and to respond to his needs. Do you have needs today? Are you backed against the wall? Disturbed and disquieted? Uncertain about your future? Anxious over a strained relationship? Burdened because someone is still without Christ? Needing extra strength, new hope, or greater wisdom? Your solution is in one word: Prayer. Tell Him every detail. Call upon the only One who can help. He awaits your request.

Read 1 Samuel 12; Matthew 7:7-11.

go for it!

How many people stop because so few say "Go"!

How few are those who see beyond the danger . . . who say to those on the edge of some venture, "*Go for it!*"

Funny, isn't it? I suppose it's related to one's inner ability to imagine, to envision, to be enraptured by the unseen, all hazards and hardships notwithstanding. I'm about convinced that one of the reasons mountain climbers connect themselves to one another with a rope is to keep the one on the end from going home. Guys out front never consider that as an option . . . but those in the rear, well, let's just say they are the last to get a glimpse of the glory. It's like a team of Huskies pulling a snowsled. The lead dog has a lot better view than the runt in the rear!

I've been thinking recently about how glad I am that certain visionaries refused to listen to the short-sighted doomsayers who could only see as far as the first obstacle. I'm glad, for example,

- that Edison didn't give up on the light bulb even though his helpers seriously doubted the thing would ever work;

- that Luther refused to back down when the Church doubled her fists and clenched her teeth;
- that Michelangelo kept pounding and painting, regardless of those negative put-downs;
- that Lindbergh decided to ignore what everyone else had said was ridiculous and was flirting with death;
- that Douglas MacArthur promised, during the darkest days of World War II, "I shall return";
- that Papa Ten Boom said yes to frightened Jews who needed a safe refuge, a hiding place;
- that the distinguished Julliard School of Music would see beyond the leg braces and wheelchair and admit an unlikely violin student named Perlman;
- that Tom Sullivan decided to be everything that he could possibly be, even though he was born blind;
- that the Gaithers made room in their busy lives for a scared young soprano named Sandi Patti who would one day thrill Christendom with "We Shall Behold Him";
- that Fred Dixon continued to train for the decathlon—and finished the course—even though critics told him he was over the hill;
- that our Lord Jesus held nothing back when He left heaven, lived on earth, and went for it—all the way to the cross—and beyond.

You could add to the list. You may even belong *on* the list. If so, hats off to you.

But there's an unfinished part to this whole idea. Almost every day—certainly every week—we encounter someone who is in his or her own homemade boat, thinking seriously about sailing on the most daring, most frightening voyage of a lifetime. That soul may be a friend, your marriage partner, someone you work with, a neighbor, perhaps a family member— your own child or brother, sister, parent. The ocean of possibilities is enormously inviting yet, let's face it, terribly threatening. Urge them on! Vote "Yes"! Shout a rousing "You are really something . . . I'm proud of you!" Dare to say what they need to hear the most, "Go for it!" Then pray like mad.

Our problem is not a lack of potential, it's a lack of perseverance . . . not a problem of having the goods but of hearing the bads. How very much could be accomplished if only there were more brave souls on the end of the pier urging us on, affirming us, regardless of the risks. People whose character is being developed, stretched, and deepened aren't hesitant to say "Go" even though the majority say "No."

William Stafford, having been asked in an interview, "When did you decide to become a poet?" responded that the question was put wrongly: "Everyone is born a poet—a person discovering the way words sound and work, caring and delighting in words. I just kept on doing what everyone starts out doing. The real question is: Why did other people stop?"

My answer: They stopped because so few said "Go!"

TODAY'S *Quest*

How easy it is to be "average." The ranks of the mediocre are crowded with status quo thinkers and predictable workers. How rare are those who live differently! Ask God to do a new work in you this day, to lift your sights above the expected, to develop in you the qualities that make for excellence. And as He lifts your sights, watch for those who may be struggling in their quest ... perhaps dangerously near giving up. May He grant you a sensitive heart and a ready word of encouragement. Say "Yes." Say "Go!"

Read Esther 4.

strong-minded determination

Stingrays have always frightened me. Not the kind you drive but the kind that swim. Having been raised near the salt water and having fished all my life, I've had numerous encounters with creatures of the sea. Most of them are fascinating to watch, fun to catch, and delicious to eat.

But stingrays? No, thanks. I don't care if Jacques Cousteau's men *do* ride on their backs, I am comfortable in only one place if those ugly, flat beasts are in the water—and that's out of the water. Perhaps that explains why the following story from a recent article in the *Los Angeles Times* immediately caught my eye.

> OCEANSIDE—It was a warm summer day in 1973, and Brian Styer was wading in shallow Pacific waters, bound for another session of surfing north of Scripps Pier in La Jolla.
>
> Suddenly, he saw a shadow moving toward him beneath the waves. It was a stingray—with a wingspan later estimated at seventeen feet. And with a lightning-quick flip of the tail, the venomous sea creature fired its sharp barb through the surfer's left kneecap and out the back of his leg.

For ten days, Styer, then eighteen, lay partially paralyzed, wondering if he would ever walk again. He did, after doctors removed a portion of the barb, declared him fit, and released him from the hospital.

But a sliver of the stingray's weaponry escaped detection by X-rays and remained lodged in Styer's knee for more than a year, causing a fierce infection that gradually invaded the surfer's entire leg, eroding muscle and bone surrounding the knee joint. He nearly lost the limb.

Twelve years and fourteen operations later, Styer is back on his board—dancing across the tops of waves with the help of a custom-made alloy brace that supports and strengthens his virtually useless knee.

And this week, after countless hours of practice, Styer realized his lifelong dream and qualified for a professional surfing contest—the world-famous Stubbies Pro International Surfing Tournament in Oceanside. His goal: To catch the eye of a sponsor and become the first disabled competitor on the pro surfing circuit.

Joining the pro tour will be no small accomplishment. For one thing, the condition of Styer's knee and the pain it causes him restrict his maneuvers and limit the length of time he can remain in the water. In addition, surfing sponsors are few, and those few may be reluctant to bet their bucks on a competitor who is 29—considered over the hill in the grueling water sport—and whose physical condition isn't 100 percent.

There is another problem. The massive doses of drugs used years ago to battle the infection creeping through Styer's body so weakened his immunity that the surfer has a 60 percent chance of contracting bacterial cancer in the leg. He is also highly susceptible to new infections, which flare up and require hospital care once every two months. A serious infection could resist treatment and force doctors to amputate.

The damage inflicted by the festering wound caused another obstacle to Styer's dreams of surfing prowess—pain. For almost ten years, the surfer relied on heavy doses of Percodan, Demerol, and other potent drugs to help him live with the pain, which is constant and is aggravated by walking, climbing stairs, and other movements.

Finally, feeling "like a vegetable" and convinced the narcotics "would kill me," Styer attended a workshop on living with pain and successfully weaned himself from the drugs. He now conducts similar pain courses at area hospitals.

These days, he relies on a wide array of measures to minimize the pain, including icing the knee, biofeedback, ultrasound, and physical therapy. And while he sleeps each night, he wears a neurostimulator that essentially blocks the electrical impulses that inform the brain of the pain in his knee.[22]

Drawing upon Styer's story, let me ask you a couple of personal questions:

First, what is your "lifelong dream"? Down deep inside your head, what hidden goal do you long to achieve? Think. State it to yourself. Picture it in your mind. The quest for character calls for a few dreams.

Second, how is your determination? Be honest. Have you started slacking off? Allowed a few obstacles to weaken your determination?

The surfer story speaks for itself, especially to me. If that guy will go through all that to accomplish his dream . . . what can I say? Bring on the stingrays, Lord!

Uh, on second thought, Lord, could You maybe strengthen me by using only *freshwater* obstacles?

In a dark moment of his life, Hudson Taylor wrote: "It doesn't matter how great the pressure is. What really matters is *where the pressure lies*—whether it comes between you and God or whether it presses you nearer His heart." Feeling the pressure today? Beginning to get the under-the-pile blues? As you pray today, shift the load from your shoulders to God's. He can handle it. He cares about you! Turn this quiet time of devotion into a pressure-release experience.

Read Psalm 18:25-36.

your niche

Linus, one of Charles Shultz's "Peanuts" tribe, often reminds me of the Rodney Dangerfield of the cartoon characters. No matter how hard he tries, how sincere, or how diligent he may be, he usually winds up looking at you as if to say, "I'll tell ya, I don't get no respect!"

In a series of cartoons some years ago the little guy was taking heat from his sister and friends for his newly found "calling"—patting little birds on the head. The distressed birds would approach Linus, lower their little feathered pates to be patted, sigh deeply, and walk away satisfied. It brought Linus no end of fulfillment—in spite of Lucy's embarrassment and chagrin.

Now I'll grant you, bird patting is a little unusual as a calling. I mean, it isn't every day you stumble across somebody who gets turned on by stroking feathers. At least we could agree that it is not one of the spiritual gifts listed in 1 Corinthians 12. Or is it? Look again.

How about that niche called "showing mercy" or "helps"? Romans 12 mentions "encouraging" and a little later "contributing to the needs of others." The more I read, the more I wonder. Who's to say that a person's niche in life couldn't be patting, stroking, and hugging?

Now if your niche *is* one of the "lesser" ones, you can expect some raised eyebrows and tongue-in-cheek comments among a few of the more sophisticated Lucy-type saints. You may even be confronted by well-meaning relatives in God's family who want to know what patting, stroking, and hugging has to do with following Christ. After all, Christianity is serious business!

In one of the scenes, Charlie Brown and Linus dialogue about all this patting. Linus wants to know, "What's wrong with patting birds on the head?" He says again that he simply wants to know what's *wrong* with it. It makes the birds feel better, it makes him feel happy all over, "So what's *wrong* with it?" Charlie stares thoughtfully, then declares rather frankly, "No one else does it!"

Some niches must struggle to exist, to say nothing of being appreciated. Not teaching. If you're a Bible teacher, wow! Superlative city. Or evangelism. No way will you be ignored or discredited. And if your thing happens to be leadership or pastoring a church or one of those up-front, get-at-it type gifts, you've got it made. Who in the world is going to "touch mine anointed"?

But wait a minute!

Let's hear it (for a change) for the "toes" on the Body. How about some applause for the "spleens" and the "tonsils" and a "fingernail" or two? I just finished reading the verse that says God has given greater honor to the lesser parts. (Read 1 Corinthians 12 for a full discussion of this.)

So if your niche is encouraging, please don't stop. If it is embracing, demonstrating warmth, compassion, and mercy to feathers that have been ruffled by offense and bruised by adversity, for goodness' sake, keep stroking. Don't quit, whatever you do. Give your heart, regardless!

If God made you a "patter," then keep on patting to the glory of God. I'll tell ya this, you've got *His* respect.

TODAY'S

Marbles or grapes, which will it be? Every congregation has a choice. You can choose to be a bag of marbles . . . independent, hard, loud, unmarked, and unaffected by others. Or you can be a bag of grapes . . . fragrant, soft, blending, mingling, flowing into one another's lives. Marbles are made to be counted and kept. Grapes are made to be bruised and used. Marbles scar and clank. Grapes yield and cling.

Read Romans 12.

ONLY WHAT WE HAVE
WROUGHT INTO OUR
CHARACTER DURING LIFE
CAN WE TAKE WITH US.
—*HUMBOLDT*

charm

So the church throughout all Judea and Galilee and Samaria enjoyed peace, being built up; and, going on in the fear of the Lord and in the comfort of the Holy Spirit, it continued to increase (Acts 9:31).

Amazing. Phenomenal, in fact. Especially when you realize the circumstances in which the church was existing at that time. Its leaders were being imprisoned. Its people were being threatened. Stephen's martyrdom was still a fresh memory (7:54-60). Paul had barely escaped with his life from the hostile Hellenistic Jews (9:28-30). A blood bath was inevitable. Yet the church throughout Palestine "enjoyed peace" and "continued to increase."

Unintimidated. Determined. Resilient.

No matter how often they were ordered to "speak no more in the name of Jesus" (5:40), they fearlessly stayed at it. Regardless of threats, warnings, floggings, and other insidious methods of persecution, the believers remained pockets of peace and places of refuge. Just imagine how infectious their enthusiasm must have been . . . how genuinely joyful!

Against all odds they flourished. Instead of shriveling into a camp of bitter, negative, and frightened people of rigid intensity, they remained winsome and magnetic. I often picture those in the early church as being people of contagious *charm*.

Whenever that mental picture appears, the insightful words of Reinhold Niebuhr come to my mind:

> You may be able to compel people to maintain certain minimum standards by stressing duty, but the highest moral and spiritual achievements depend not upon a push but a pull. People must be charmed into righteousness.[23]

When will today's church ever learn this? How much longer must we rely on pushing and demanding? What will it take to bring back the charm . . . that marvelous grace which draws righteousness out of us like iron shavings to a massive magnet? Somehow the early saints maintained a loving atmosphere, an authentic appeal of positive acceptance. No amount of pressure from without disturbed the peace within. The result was predictable: People could not stay away from their meeting places. The assembly of believers was *the* place to be . . . to be yourself . . . to share your grief . . . to ask your questions . . . to admit your needs . . . to shed your tears . . . to speak your mind . . . to dream your dreams. Why, of course! Is there any place on earth more suitable, more perfectly designed for that kind of openness?

Blind songwriter Ken Medema captured the scene when he wrote:

> If this is not a place where tears are under-
>   stood
>   Then where shall I go to cry?
> And if this is not a place where my spirit can
>   take wings
>   Then where shall I go to fly?
> I don't need another place
>   for tryin' to impress you
> With just how good and virtuous I am,
>   no, no, no.
> I don't need another place
>   for always bein' on top of things
> Everybody knows that it's a sham,
>   it's a sham.
> I don't need another place
>   for always wearin' smiles
> Even when it's not the way I feel.
> I don't need another place
>   to mouth the same old platitudes
> Everybody knows that it's not real.
> So if this is not a place where my questions
>   can be asked
>   Then where shall I go to seek?
> And if this is not a place where my heart cry
>   can be heard
>   Where, tell me where, shall I go to speak?[24]

Wouldn't it be wonderful if in some future day a historian, looking back on our times, might write:

So the church throughout all America and Canada and Mexico enjoyed peace, being built up . . . it continued to increase. An irresistible magnet drew people in. The quest for character held them close.

It will require one all-pervasive ingredient if that entry will ever find its way into tomorrow's chronicle of church history: charm.

When the early Church met, magnetic charm brought joy. When they prayed, there was power. When they gave, there was generosity. When they embraced, there was love. When they spoke, there was authenticity. When they left, there were tears. Nineteen centuries later, the Church continues. Our family is much bigger and more influential. But is it better? Think that over as you pause in His presence today.

Read Acts 4.

wise compromise

During a critical period in my growing-up years I was exposed to bad counsel. Being too naive to know the difference, too gullible to discern error, and therefore too weak to resist, I bit off the whole enchilada. Color me dogmatic back then ... judgmental, extreme, borderline fanatical. I was sincere and young, but wrong.

It was bad enough to be so rigid so early in my life, but when I think of the damage it created in relationships, the doors it closed to opportunities, and the deadness it caused in my spiritual growth, I am still chagrined. Maybe you spent some of your years in the same scene. If so, you'll have no difficulty identifying with that part of my pilgrimage. If not, a little explanation might help.

In the ranks of twentieth-century Christianity, there is a pocket of people who take pride in being ultra whatever. Conservative to the core and opinionated to the point of distraction, these folks are not open to discuss crucial issues nor even to *hear* the ideas from the other side. To them, that kind of tolerance is tantamount to contamination—an outright and dangerous acceptance of evil. In order to maintain purity and to guard against any subtle inroad of heresy, they simply refuse to think outside the boundaries of certain self-imposed rules and regulations. Strict adherence to this mindset results in acceptance by "the group," which gives tremendous feelings of safety and security . . . a tragic syndrome.

The tragedy is intensified by the use of certain scriptures that seem to encourage such closed-minded convictions. Those verses (more often than not half-verses or passages wrenched from context) are repeated over and over again until everybody marches in step and nobody has the audacity to call anything into question. In place of the strong and needed traditions that give us purpose and roots, there is superimposed a weak traditionalism that leaves no room for thinking or questioning.

Jaroslav Pelikan put it well:

Tradition is the living faith of those now dead. Traditionalism is the dead faith of those still living.[25]

As I think back to that era in my life, one of the key terms was *compromise*. It was always presented in a bad light. If you listened to people outside the camp, you might be influenced by them . . . which would lead to compromise. If you didn't agree with the guru who called all the shots (yes, all), then it was clear that you were compromising with the truth. If you failed to keep "the list" exactly as the group dictated—regardless of the lack of biblical support for such a list—then, clearly, you were guilty of compromise. Funny, nobody was ever able to state the original source of such a list, but there was no doubt about compromise if you broke even one of those rules. This is the worst kind of bondage, because it is all done under the guise of Christianity.

Enough negatives. My point here is that compromise is not always bad. Obviously, there are moral and ethical standards overtly taught in Scripture which leave no room whatsoever for compromise. But compromise is much broader than that. Sometimes it's wise to compromise. In your quest for character, don't miss this vital, rare quality!

Without compromise, disagreements cannot be settled. So negotiations grind to a halt. A marriage is maintained and strengthened by compromise as is the relationship between parent and child. Moms and dads who have no wobble room are asking for trouble when the teenage years surface. Siblings who will not compromise fight. Congregations who will not compromise on important issues that have two sides split. Nations with differing ideologies that refuse to listen to each other and won't compromise at various points go to war. Neighbors that won't compromise sue.

Am I saying it's easy? Or free from risk? Or that it comes naturally? No. It is much easier (and safer) to stand your ground . . . to keep on believing that your way is the way to go and that your plan is the plan to follow. One major problem however . . . you wind up narrow-minded and alone, or surrounded by a few nonthinkers who resemble the miniature plastic dog in the back window of the car, always nodding yes.

That may be safe, but it doesn't seem very satisfying. Or Christlike. While pursuing true character, don't miss wise compromise. C'mon, give your heart permission to flex!

One final observation: Those who master this art are seldom very young. With youth comes more idealism and less realism; loud dogmatism instead of quiet tolerance. The poet, Sara Teasdale, understood:

> When I have ceased to break my wings
> Against the faultiness of things,
> And learned that compromises wait
> Behind each hardly opened gate,
> When I can look Life in the eyes,
> Grown calm and very coldly wise,
> Life will have given me the Truth
> And taken in exchange—my youth.[26]

Ponder these penetrating words as you quiet yourself before Him today ... words I never once heard emphasized in my growing-up years:

> *Do nothing from selfishness or empty conceit, but with humility of mind let each of you regard one another as more important than himself; do not merely look out for your own personal interests, but also for the interests of others* (Philippians 2:3-4).

contentment

Everybody says they want it, but most people run right by it.

Contentment is the lonely hitchhiker reflected in the rearview mirror as the transfixed driver hurdles by on the expressway. Few bother to notice they've sped past the very thing they kept saying they were looking for. And even if they did notice a blurred object in their peripheral vision, there was really no time to slow down and investigate. It went by too fast. And the traffic speeds on.

Books on contentment decorate the windows of a thousand bookstores. And keep right on selling. Isn't it strange that we need a *book* to help us experience what ought to come naturally? No, not really. Not when you've been programmed to compete, achieve, increase, fight, and worry your way up the so-called "ladder of success" (which few can even define). Not when you've worshiped at the shrine of PROMOTION since adolescence. Not when you've served all your life as a galley slave on the ship of *Public Opinion*. To you, contentment is the unknown "X" in life's equation. It is as strange to you as living in an igloo or as unheard-of as raising a rhinoceros in your backyard.

Face it. You and I are afraid that if we open the door of contentment, two belligerent guests will rush in—loss of prestige and laziness. We really believe that "getting to the top" is worth *any* sacrifice. To proud Americans, contentment is something to be enjoyed between birth and kindergarten, retirement and the rest home, or (this may hurt) among "those who have no ambition."

Stop and think. A young man with keen mechanical skills and little interest in academics is often counseled against being contented to settle for a trade right out of high school. A teacher who is competent, contented, and fulfilled in the classroom is frowned upon if she turns down an offer to become a principal. The owner of *El Pollo Loco* on the corner has a packed-out joint every day—and is happy in his soul, contented in his spirit. But chances are, selfish ambition won't let him rest until he opens ten other places and gets rich—leaving contentment in the lower drawer of forgotten dreams. A man who serves as an assistant—or any support personnel in a ministry, company, or the military—frequently wrestles with feelings of discontent until he or she is promoted to the top rung of the scale—regardless of personal capabilities.

Illustrations are legion. This applies to mothers, homemakers, or nuclear scientists, plumbers or cops, engineers or seminary students, caretakers or carpet layers, artists or waitresses. This ridiculous pattern would be hilarious if it weren't so tragic . . . and common. Small wonder so many get frostbitten amidst the winter of their discontent.

"Striving to better, oft we mar what's well," wrote Shakespeare. It's a curious fact that when people are free to do as they please, they usually imitate each other. I seriously fear we are rapidly becoming a nation of discontented, incompetent marionettes, dangling from strings manipulated by the same, dictatorial puppeteer.

Listen to John the Baptist: "*. . . be content with your wages*" (Luke 3:14).

Hear Paul: "*I am well content with weaknesses : . . if we have food and covering . . . be content!* (2 Corinthians 12:10, 1 Timothy 6:8).

And another apostle: "*. . . let your character be free . . . being content with what you have*" (Hebrews 13:5).

Now I warn you—this isn't easy to implement. You'll be outnumbered and outvoted. You'll have to fight the urge to conform. Even the greatest of all apostles admitted, "I have learned to be content" (Philippians 4:11). It *is* a learning process, often quite painful. And it isn't very enjoyable marching out of step until you are convinced you are listening to the right drummer.

When you are fully convinced, a new dimension of your character will take shape. And as that occurs, two things will happen: (1) Your strings will be cut, and (2) you'll be free, indeed! And surprise! You'll find that lonely hitchhiker you left miles back sitting in the passenger seat right beside you . . . smiling every mile of the way.

When Jesus spoke of the things that choke the truth of God's Word from our lives, He mentioned three specifics: worry, money, and discontentment (Mark 4:19). Read the three again. Ask the Lord to speak to you today about any or all of these things . . . and as He does, to "unchoke" your life. Only then can you know the full joy of His companionship.

Read Mark 4:1-20.

things that don't change

A long-time friend and mentor of mine died yesterday. He was a preacher *par excellence.* Trained in the old school. Always in a shirt and tie—with knot slim and tight. Three-piece suit, preferably. White shirt, well-pressed, heavy on the starch. Shoes shined. Every hair in place. Cleanly shaven. Trim. Immaculately tailored. And beneath all those externals? Character, solid as a stone.

His style of delivery? Strong. Dogmatic at times. Eloquent, often. Lots of alliteration with a memorized poem toward the end. Laced with illustrations that often began, "The story is told . . ." Never much humor, always dignified, a bit aloof, mystical, deep in thought, a voice in the lower register. Lots of leather-bound volumes in his library. Determined to hold high his call into ministry. Olive skin, deep eyes, straight teeth. Confident yet not arrogant. Handsome but not vain.

Never a hint of silly frivolity. Not the kind of man you'd expect to sit cross-legged in the front yard messing around with the kids. Or in the kitchen doing the dishes. Or changing the oil in his car. Or trying a back flip off the high dive. Or playing one-on-one in the driveway. The man had class.

It isn't that he was above all that, it's just that in his day, ministry-types maintained a sharp, straight edge. If he wasn't preaching, he was getting ready to. If he wasn't praying, he had just finished. Frankly, I was never in his presence without feeling a sense of awe. Though a grown man, I sat up straight in his study and said "Sir" a lot. When he put his hand on my shoulder and prayed that God would "guide this young man" and "set him apart for the Master's use," I felt as if I had been knighted. He dripped with integrity. His counsel proved invincible. His thought and words were pristine pure—crisp and clean as a nun's habit. When he stepped behind a pulpit, he stood like a ram-rod, polished and poised—surely one of the best in his day. he could have posed for the "Gentleman's Psalm" . . . Psalm 15.

But much of "his day" has passed. Today's approach with people is so very different. His was the era of Walter Winchell, George Patton, and Norman Rockwell. The no-monkey-business philosophy where lines were sharp, clearly defined, and speeches were one-way addresses. Dialogue was unheard of . . . the vulnerability of leaders? *Anathema.* How times have changed! There isn't a profession that hasn't been forced to shift, making room for changes that are inevitable, many of them essential.

I thought of that recently while reading the following job description given to floor nurses by a hospital in 1887. You who are nurses and physicians will smile in disbelief.

NURSES' DUTIES IN 1887

In addition to caring for your fifty patients, each nurse will follow these regulations:

1. Daily sweep and mop the floors of your ward, dust the patient's furniture and window sills.

2. Maintain an even temperature in your ward by bringing in a scuttle of coal for the day's business.

3. Light is important to observe the patient's condition. Therefore, each day fill kerosene lamps, clean chimneys, and trim wicks. Wash the windows once a week.

4. The nurse's notes are important in aiding the physician's work. Make your pens carefully; you may whittle nibs to your individual taste.

5. Each nurse on day duty will report every day at 7 A.M. and leave at 8 P.M., except on the Sabbath, on which day you will be off from 12 noon to 2 P.M.

6. Graduate nurses in good standing with the director of nurses will be given an evening off each week for courting purposes or two evenings a week if you go regularly to church.

7. Each nurse should lay aside from each payday a goodly sum of her earnings for her benefits during her declining years so that she will not become a burden. For example, if you earn $30 a month, you should set aside $15.

8. Any nurse who smokes, uses liquor in any form, gets her hair done at a beauty shop, or frequents dance halls will give the director of nurses good reason to suspect her worth, intentions, and integrity.

9. The nurse who performs her labors and serves her patients and doctors faithfully and without fault for a period of five years will be given an increase by the hospital administration of five cents a day, providing there are no hospital debts that are outstanding.

Anybody else glad there have been some changes since 1887?

Yes, times do change things — sometimes drastically. Styles change, as do expectations, salaries, communication systems, relating to people, even preaching techniques.

But some things have no business changing. Like respect for authority, personal integrity, wholesome thoughts, pure words, holy living, distinct roles of masculinity and femininity, commitment to Christ, love for family, and authentic servanthood. Character qualities are never up for grabs.

My friend and mentor is gone. Much of his style has left with him. But the deep-down stuff that made him great—ah, may that never be forgotten. Times must change. But character? Not on your life . . . or death.

TODAY'S Quest

Life? "A vapor," answers James 4:14. "As uncertain as the morning fog" (The Living Bible). "Like a puff of smoke" (Phillips). Although we give the appearance of security, our lives are marked by uncertainty, adversity, brevity. All the more reason to gain perspective on how to live it. Walking with God does that. It doesn't guarantee we'll live longer, but it does help us live better. And deeper. And broader. Since you know nothing about the day, week, or year before you, commit yourself anew to Him who knows the times and the seasons.

Read James 4.

true teamwork

John Stemmons, a well-known Dallas businessman, was asked to make a brief statement on what he considered to be foundational to developing a good team. His answer was crisp and clear. It is worth repeating.

> Find some people who are comers, who are going to be achievers in their own field . . . and people you can trust. Then grow old together.

Want a good illustration of that? The Billy Graham evangelistic team, the inner core of those greathearted, gifted people whose names are now legend. As I looked into the faces of most of them in our church last Sunday, shook their hands, and felt warmed by their gracious smiles, it dawned on me that I cannot remember when they *weren't* together. It's almost as if they were born into the same family—or at least reared in the same neighborhood. In a day of job-hopping and a Lone Ranger religious mentality, it is refreshing to see such a group of capable and dedicated people, each one different and distinct, growing old together, yet still very much a solid team.

Don't misread what it means to be a team. Group loyalty is not blind allegiance or harboring incompetence.

Neither is it nepotistic prejudice which conveys the idea that everyone else is wrong except our little group. Nor is it so exclusive and so proud that it appears closed and secretive. Rather, there is freedom to be, to develop, to innovate, to make mistakes, to learn from one another . . . all the while feeling loved, supported, and affirmed. Such a context has been called "management by friendship." Instead of suspicion and put-downs, there is trust that builds an *esprit de corps* within the team. Stress is held to a minimum since affection flows and laughter is encouraged. Who doesn't develop strong character in a secure scene like that?

In his best-seller, *American Caesar*, William Manchester introduces his readers to an in-depth acquaintance with Douglas MacArthur. He helps us feel closer to that strong personality as he digs beneath the intimidating exterior and unveils many of MacArthur's magnetic characteristics as well as strange quirks. At one point, the author analyzes the remarkable loyalty which Colonel MacArthur elicited from his troops during World War I. By the time that war had ended, the man had won seven Silver Stars, two Distinguished Service Crosses, and also the coveted Distinguished Service Medal.

Obviously, those medals were partly due to his own bravery, but it cannot be denied that they were also due to another factor: his ability to educe a fierce loyalty from the men under his command. How did he pull that off? Here is Manchester's analysis in a nutshell:

- He was closer to their age than the other senior officers.
- He shared their discomforts and their danger.
- He adored them in return.[27]

Regardless of the man's well-publicized egomania and emotional distortions, MacArthur possessed a major redeeming virtue that eclipsed his flaws in his men's eyes and fired their passions: He genuinely and deeply cared for them. The word is *love*. Nothing . . . absolutely nothing pulls a team closer together or strengthens the lines of loyalty more than love. It breaks down internal competition. It silences gossip. It builds morale. It promotes feelings that say, "I belong" and "Who cares who gets the credit?" and "I must do my very best" and "You can trust me because I trust you."

Jesus' team of disciples was hardly the epitome of success when they got started together. One would have wondered then why He selected such "a ragged aggregation of souls,"[28] as Robert Coleman tagged them. The genius of His plan was not immediately obvious. But by the end of the first century, no one would fault His selection. Except for the deceiver, they were "comers," they proved themselves "achievers in their own field," and they became "people you can trust." Ultimately, they were responsible for turning their world upside down . . . or should I say right-side up? Whichever, no group in history has proven itself more effective than that first-century evangelistic team, the inner core of Christ's men.

I haven't a clue why I was prompted to write these things today, only a strong sense of urgency to do so. Maybe you are in the process of putting together a group—a special team of people to accomplish some significant objectives. Here's a tip worth remembering: Instead of just going for big names or starting with a few hotshots, look for some comers, achievers in process, truly trustworthy folks . . . love 'em to their full potential as you cultivate a long-haul friendship. Give your heart in unrestrained affection! Then watch God work. A team drawn together by love and held together by grace has staying power.

I suppose we could call that growing old gracefully.

Before you look down at the hymnal next Sunday in your worship service, look around. Most of the people you will see are your brothers and sisters in the family of God. You need them. They need you. Independent and separate, you are weak. So are they. But together, all of you form one strong unit . . . capable of weathering storms outside the church walls. As you pray today, give the Father thanks that you are not alone in this rugged journey from earth to heaven.

Read 1 Corinthians 12.

dedication

Rare indeed are those folk who give of themselves with little regard for recognition, personal benefit, or monetary returns.

For some reason we are slowly eroding into a people that gauges every request for involvement from the viewpoint: *"What do I get out of it?"* or *"How can I get the most for the least?"* Tucked underneath that philosophy is a tremendous loss of plain old American dedication. Thanks to our lazy natures, we do not feel very uncomfortable getting by with the least amount of effort. Our former drive for excellence and quality control is now sacrificed on the altar of such rationalizations as:

"Well, nobody's perfect."
"That's good enough to get by."
"Don't worry, no one will even notice."
"Everybody's doing it."

As a result, our standard has become *mediocrity* and our goal, *maintaining the average.* The consecrated worker, the high achiever, the dedicated employee, the student who strives for excellence is often labeled a neurotic or shunned as a fanatic.

I find more encouragement from God's Word than any other source of information when it comes to the importance of personal dedication. The Lord assures me that His *glory* is my goal (1 Corinthians 10:31), not man's approval. Furthermore, when He tells me to love, He tells me to do it *fervently* (1 Peter 4:8). When maintaining a friendship, it is to be *devotedly* (Romans 12:10). When steering clear of evil, I am told to stay away from even *the appearance* of it (1 Thessalonians 5:22). When seeing a brother or sister in need, we are to bear his or her burden *sacrificially* (Galatians 6:1-2), not stay at a safe distance. When it comes to work, we are to be *disciplined* (2 Thessalonians 3:7-8) and *diligent* (1 Thessalonians 2:9). The Scriptures are replete with exhortations to go above and beyond the required call of duty—to a dedication of life that thrives on the challenge of doing a quality piece of work.

Lest you think this is too severe, I close with an excerpt from an actual letter written by a young communist to his fiancee, breaking off their engagement. The girl's pastor sent the letter to Billy Graham, who published it a number of years ago.

The communist student wrote:

> *We communists have a high casualty rate. We are the ones who get shot and hung and ridiculed and fired from our jobs and in every other way made as uncomfortable as possible. A certain percentage of us get killed or imprisoned. We live in virtual poverty. We turn back to the party every penny we make above what is absolutely necessary to keep us alive.*

We communists do not have the time or the money for many movies, or concerts, or T-bone steaks, or decent homes, or new cars. We have been described as fanatics. We are fanatics. Our lives are dominated by one great overshadowing factor: the struggle for world communism. We communists have a philosophy of life which no amount of money can buy. We have a cause to fight for, a definite purpose in life. We subordinate our petty personal selves into a great movement of humanity; and if our personal lives seem hard or our egos appear to suffer through subordination to the party, then we are adequately compensated by the thought that each of us in his small way is contributing to something new and true and better for mankind.

There is one thing which I am in dead earnest about, and that is the communist cause. It is my life, my business, my religion, my hobby, my sweetheart, my wife, my mistress, and my bread and meat. I work at it in the daytime and dream of it at night. Its hold on me grows, not lessens, as time goes on; therefore, I cannot carry on a friendship, a love affair, or even a conversation without relating it to this force which both drives and guides my life. I evaluate people, looks, ideas, and actions according to how they affect the communist cause, and by their attitude toward it. I've already been in jail because of my ideals, and if necessary, I'm ready to go before a firing squad.

That, my friend, is total dedication. The quest for character must include this rare, essential trait. Don't be afraid of it! Such commitment to excellence is not only rare, it's downright contagious.

TODAY'S Quest

Need a fresh and challenging goal? Read Isaiah 58. Concentrate on verse 12. Consider the possibility of filling these three roles: a "rebuilder," a "repairer," a "restorer." All three are yours for the taking. During a few moments of quietness, ask God for a sensitive heart to those around you. Thank Him for rebuilding, repairing, and restoring you. Tell Him you are all His—no conditions, no exceptions, no reservations.

dreaming

Tom Fatjo is into garbage.

Oh, he hasn't always been. He used to be a quiet, efficient accounting executive. Another of those prim and proper Rice University grads who was going to play it straight, dodge all risk, and settle down easily into a life of the predictable. Boring but stable. Safe. Everything was running along as planned until that night Tom found himself surrounded by a roomful of angry homeowners. As he sat among all those irritated people at the Willowbrook Civic Club in the south-western section of Houston, his internal wheels began to turn.

You see, the city had refused to pick up their garbage at the back door of their homes. They had hired a private company to do it, but now that company was having serious problems. So the garbage was starting to stack up. And flies were everywhere, which only added to the sticky misery of that hot south Texas summer. Heated words flashed across the room.

And that night Tom Fatjo couldn't sleep.

A crazy idea kept rolling around in his head. A dream too unreal to admit to anyone but himself. A dream that spawned a series of incredible thoughts. That resulted in the purchase of a garbage truck. That led to a ten-year adventure you'd have trouble believing. That evolved into the largest solid-waste disposal company in the world, Browning-Ferris Industries, Inc. With annual sales in excess of (are you ready for this?)$500 *million*. And that was only the beginning. Tom has also been instrumental in building over ten other companies—large companies—like the Criterion Capital Corporation, whose subsidiaries and affiliates manage well over $2 *billion*.

And to think it all started with a garbage truck.

No, a dream.

An unthinkable, scary, absolutely wild idea that refused to let him sleep. Getting up quietly so as not to awaken his wife Diane, or his daughter, he sat down and stared out the window at the high, white moon. Just listen to his words:

> At the time we were living on $750 a month. My partners and I had agreed when we started our accounting firm to conserve by living on reduced income, so I could certainly use some extra money. Increased income and solving the subdivision's garbage problems were my goals. Next, I listed the financial information I would need to see if going into the garbage business would be feasible. I daydreamed some more about being a garbage man, and laughed out loud as I pictured the look on people's faces when they heard that conservative Tom Fatjo with the white shirts and dark suits was driving a garbage truck. But excitement about

doing this was much deeper than the allure of doing something different. I didn't know exactly why, but this crazy idea was suddenly very important to me.[29]

That's the way it is with dreams. Especially when God is in them. They appear crazy (they *are* crazy!). Placed alongside the equiangular triangle of logic, cost, and timing, dreams are never congruent. They won't fly when you test them against the gravity of reality. And the strangest part of all: the more they are told "can't," the more they pulsate "can" and "will" and "must."

What's behind great accomplishments? Inevitably, great people. But what is in those "great people" that makes them different? It's certainly not their age or sex or color or heritage or environment. No, it's got to be something inside their heads. They are people who *think* differently. People whose ideas are woven into a meaningful pattern on the loom of dreams, threaded with colorful strands of imagination, creativity, even a touch of fantasy. They are among that band of young men the Scripture mentions "who will dream dreams and see visions."

But there is another band of equally great people—they are the ones *married* to those modern day seers! My counsel to you is this: Give the dreamers room. Go easy on the "shouldn'ts" and the "can'ts," okay? Dreams are fragile things that have a hard time emerging in a cloud of negativism, reminders like "no money," and "too many problems." Have patience.

Yours is a special calling. In fact, you're a partner in the process . . . so stay ready for anything. And I mean anything!

Whatever a dreamer gets into, so does his wife. Just be glad you're not a lady named Diane, who is expected to get into what her husband's into.

Growth, though silent as light, is one of the practical proofs of health. This is certainly true in the spiritual realm. And the result of growth in Christ? Fruit. Read John 15, then go back and carefully reread verses 1-7. "No fruit. Fruit. More fruit. Much fruit." Where are *you* on that spectrum? Think about your growth and the measure of your fruit as you spend time with the Lord today.

caricatures

Most of us don't realize the caricatures, the ludicrous and distorted mental pictures folks have of church-going, Bible-toting "saints."

It's true. We represent a host of spooky, hard-to-understand concepts.

We refer to being "born again" even though we reject reincarnation. That's *strange* to the uninitiated. We talk out loud to a Person we cannot see, and we commit our entire future to One we've never met because a Book we believe He wrote (though we didn't see Him do it) tells us that we should. That's quite a dose for some to swallow. We say we are followers of Christ, but there are a few times every year we act like the devil. We claim to be citizens of heaven, but we walk around on earth. We talk about love and forgiveness, purity, and compassion, but we murder with our mouths, lust with our eyes, and ignore with our ears.

You and I understand those contrasts because we have been carefully instructed, we have learned about the carnal-spiritual battle. So we leave room for such contradictions . . . but the guy outside doesn't. He mentally constructs a distorted conglomeration of things that are a mixture of exaggertion, confusion, and fact. The world sees us rip off one another and pictures us with two faces and a forked tongue. In a weak or hurried moment, we make a couple of stupid statements—so an empty head is added to the caricature. I don't know how many people have told me that a major battle before becoming a Christian was the fear of having to commit intellectual suicide. We nod in agreement that "it is better to give than to receive," then spend our days grabbing and grasping—so our hands are oversized and our eyes are bulging with greed. How rare are the authentic models of Christian character!

Our worry list is long though we say He takes our burdens . . . our patience with the waitress is short even though she saw us pray . . . our driving is often somewhere between irritating thoughtlessness and rank lawlessness even though that bumper sticker identifies us as people who model the gospel message. Color us red. Rather than that, give us masks. Better still, *make us invisible*!

Caricatures, admittedly, are false freaks, extreme representations. But they cause formidable hangups when the subject of Christianity is brought up. The cross is supposed to be offensive, remember, not the Christian. The death and resurrection of Christ have sufficient power to penetrate like a double-edged razor. Like it or not, fake models dull the edges.

The answer is not to try really hard to be perfect (waste of time) or to peel off the "Jesus Is Lord" sticker (cop out) or to keep apologizing (guilt trip) so all caricatures might be erased. Face it, some folks wouldn't change their erroneous ideas about Christians even if every one of us were suddenly more devoted than John the Baptist. Furthermore, the life of faith and our deeply significant convictions are not suspect because the majority in our day choose to walk by sight and mock those who don't.

Then what's the point? You can't change the model of other Christians. And you can't change the mind of other non-Christians. But you can do something about the lack of character inside *your* skin.

The presence of caricatures doesn't matter nearly so much as the absence of character.

Paul's intense desire in life was: "That I may know Him—that I may progressively become more deeply and intimately acquainted with Him, perceiving and recognizing and understanding [the wonders of His person] more strongly and clearly" (Philippians 3:10, The Amplified Bible). What is yours? Think it over.

Read Philippians 3.

GOD IS MORE CONCERNED
ABOUT OUR CHARACTER
THAN OUR COMFORT.

HIS GOAL IS NOT
TO PAMPER US PHYSICALLY
BUT TO PERFECT US
SPIRITUALLY.
　　　　　—PAUL W. POWELL

the gift that lives on

In our pocket of society where pampered affluence is rampant, we are often at a loss to know what kind of gifts to buy our friends and loved ones on special occasions. For some people (especially those who "have everything") the standard type gift won't cut it. Nothing in the shopping mall catches our fancy.

I have a suggestion. It may not seem that expensive or sound very novel, but believe me, it works every time. It's one of those gifts that has great value but no price tag. It can't be lost nor will it ever be forgotten. No problem with size either. It fits all shapes, any age, and every personality. This ideal gift is . . . *yourself*. In your quest for character, don't forget the value of unselfishness.

That's right, give some of yourself away.

Give an hour of your time to someone who needs you. Give a note of encouragement to someone who is down. Give a hug of affirmation to someone in your family. Give a visit of mercy to someone who is laid aside. Give a meal you prepared to someone who is sick. Give a word of compassion to someone who just lost a mate. Give a deed of kindness to someone who is slow and easily overlooked. Jesus taught: ". . . to the extent that you did it to one of these brothers of Mine, even the least of them, you did it to Me" (Matthew 25:40).

Teddy Stallard certainly qualified as "one of the least." Disinterested in school. Musty, wrinkled clothes; hair never combed. One of those kids in school with a deadpan face, expressionless—sort of a glassy, unfocused stare. When Miss Thompson spoke to Teddy he always answered in monosyllables. Unattractive, unmotivated, and distant, he was just plain hard to like. Even though his teacher said she loved all in her class the same, down inside she wasn't being completely truthful.

Whenever she marked Teddy's papers, she got a certain perverse pleasure out of putting *X*'s next to the wrong answers and when she put the *F*'s at the top of the papers, she always did it with a flair. She should have known better; she had Teddy's records and she knew more about him than she wanted to admit. The records read:

1st   Grade: *Teddy shows promise with his work and attitude, but poor home situation.*
2nd Grade: *Teddy could do better. Mother is seriously ill. He receives little help at home.*
3rd Grade: *Teddy is a good boy but too serious. He is a slow learner. His mother died this year.*
4th Grade: *Teddy is very slow, but well-behaved. His father shows no interest.*

Christmas came and the boys and girls in Miss Thompson's class brought her Christmas presents. They piled their presents on her desk and crowded around to watch her open them. Among the presents there was one from Teddy Stallard. She was surprised that he had brought her a gift, but he had. Teddy's gift was wrapped in brown paper and was held together with Scotch tape. On the paper were written the simple words, "For Miss Thompson from Teddy." When she opened Teddy's present, out fell a gaudy rhinestone bracelet, with half the stones missing, and a bottle of cheap perfume.

The other boys and girls began to giggle and smirk over Teddy's gifts, but Miss Thompson at least had enough sense to silence them by immediately putting on the bracelet and putting some of the perfume on her wrist. Holding her wrist up for the other children to smell, she said, "Doesn't it smell lovely?" And the children, taking their cue from the teacher, readily agreed with "oo's" and "ah's."

At the end of the day, when school was over and the other children had left, Teddy lingered behind. He slowly came over to her desk and said softly, "Miss Thompson . . . Miss Thompson, you smell just like my mother . . . and her bracelet looks real pretty on you, too. I'm glad you liked my presents." When Teddy left, Miss Thompson got down on her knees and asked God to forgive her.

The next day when the children came to school, they were welcomed by a new teacher. Miss Thompson had become a different person. She was no longer just a teacher; she had become an agent of God. She was now a person committed to loving her children and doing things for them that would live on after her. She helped all the children, but especially the slow ones, and especially Teddy Stallard. By the end of that school year, Teddy showed dramatic improvement. He had caught up with most of the students and was even ahead of some.

She didn't hear from Teddy for a long time. Then one day, she received a note that read:

Dear Miss Thompson:
I wanted you to be the first to know.
I will be graduating second in my class.
Love,
Teddy Stallard

Four years later, another note came:

Dear Miss Thompson:
They just told me I will be graduating first in my class. I wanted you to be the first to know. The university has not been easy, but I liked it.
Love,
Teddy Stallard

And four years later:

Dear Miss Thompson:
As of today, I am Theodore Stallard, M.D. How about that? I wanted you to be the first to know. I am getting married next month, the 27th to be exact. I want you to come and sit where my mother would sit if she were alive. You are the only family I have now; Dad died last year.
Love,
Teddy Stallard

Miss Thompson went to that wedding and sat where Teddy's mother would have sat. She deserved to sit there; she had done something for Teddy that he could never forget.[30]

What can *you* give as a gift? Instead of giving only something you buy, risk giving something that will live on after you. Be really generous. Give yourself to a Teddy Stallard, "one of the least," whom you can help to become one of the greats.

TODAY'S *Quest*

Love. No greater theme can be emphasized. No stronger message can be proclaimed. No finer song can be sung. No better truth can be imagined. "O, the deep, deep love of Jesus!" Let that be your theme, your song, your every thought today as you worship the Son.

Read 1 John 2:7-10, 3:13-24.

a time for truth

"Jus' gimme the facts, ma'am; all I want are the facts."

Dum da dum dum. Dum da dum dum—*duuum*!

His name, you may remember, was Friday, Sergeant Friday of the Los Angeles Police Department. Hard-boiled. Tight-lipped. Thick-skinned. Those beady eyes. That steel-trap mind. Wherever he went, whatever he did, it was always "the facts" that he wanted. Those questions, those staccato-like words, were designed to draw them out. Humor, suspense, surprise, even a touch of romance may have been woven through the story line, but none of those things ever got the hero of TV's *Dragnet* off target. He was forever in hot pursuit of one thing and one thing only—*facts*.

Today Jack Webb's mug is but a memory. He was the first, but certainly not the last of exciting and adventurous tube detectives. Since Friday faded, we've seen Kojak, Mannix, Rockford, McGarrett, Barnaby Jones, Matt Houston, Mike Hammer, Thomas Magnum, and other hard-nosed types who wear blue on Hill Street and fight vice in Miami. But they all have one thing in common. To solve the crime, each one needs the same thing. The only thing that will put the puzzle together and ultimately stand up in court. Facts.

There is something comforting about facts. Something wonderfully settling and secure, even relieving. Churchill's comment comes to mind:

> I pass with relief from the tossing sea of Cause and Theory to the firm ground of Result and Fact.[31]

I shall never forget a classroom setting that occurred about twenty-five years ago. As usual, I was in the front row. One of the toughest professors in graduate school tossed out a question. Eager and over zealous, I jumped in prematurely. He let me continue until it was obvious that my position was growing thinner by the second. He stared through me, frowned, then replied, "Mr. Swindoll, if you continue any further out on that weak limb, I'm going to saw you off with a hard set of facts." I can still feel the teeth in that mental saw of his. He was notorious around the campus as a prof who had little room for feelings, only facts. Stubborn, irresistible, undeniable facts. I feared him then. Today, my fear has been replaced with respect.

In a day of overemphasis on feelings, especially in religious circles, a return to some facts seems overdue. Not the kind of facts where people sit around and munch on theological trivia or argue about biblical data no one can use or even needs to know. But facts that bring confidence and give reassurance. Solid, foundational, essential truth that makes us courageous when storm clouds gather. And, friend, they *have* gathered.

A firm grip on essential biblical facts is like a steady hand on the tiller as the wind whips the water around you into whitecaps. Where do we find these vital truths? In God's Word. And how do we get started? Here are several suggestions.

- Join with one or two others in a weekly study of a book in the Bible or the basic doctrines. Ask your pastor or the folks at your local Christian bookstore for help in getting your hands on *readable, reliable* books or self-study material.
- Enroll in an evening school class or two at the nearest Bible college—or check into the possibility of pursuing a good correspondence course.
- Get into a "read through the Bible program" that keeps you in the Word day in and day out. Invite a friend to join you in this daily journey and check in on one another's progress each week. Research shows it takes at least three to four weeks for an activity to become habit.

As this life-giving flow of truth surges through your spiritual veins, you will find yourself less intimidated in the storm and better able to navigate through the clouds. It is not a dramatic overstatement for me to add that you will stand taller and think clearer as you gather and arrange these biblical facts in your arsenal of logic.

Best of all, you will become distinctly different, a rare find in our day: a Christian with courage . . . a believer who is growing and learning in your walk with Christ.

Aleksandr Solzhenitsyn's words haunt me:

> Must one point out that from ancient times a decline in courage has been considered the beginning of the end?[32]

We still need each other. We still need to relate, to feel, to enjoy our Lord, to sing His praises. Yes . . . more than ever.

But I believe we also need to know what we believe. And why we believe it. That takes a solid framework of truth fitted together in an impenetrable network of facts. It's time for the truth to be told as it relates to our doctrinal roots. The Christian's "decline in courage" is becoming all too obvious.

Let's encourage each other on this crucial quest. We believers need to get our facts straight as never before. The last thing any of us need is to be out on a weak limb!

Q TODAY'S uest

Who can possibly measure the lasting impact of the Word of God? In a world without standards, where everything is relative, where the pace is maddening, and prices are soaring, there is great security in opening God's timeless Book and hearing His voice. It calms our fears. It clears our heads. It comforts our hearts. It corrects our walk. It confirms our commitment. Let it have its entrance today. Say what young Samuel once said, "Speak, for Thy servant is listening."

Read Deuteronomy 30:11-14.

gumption

We don't hear much about gumption any more. Too bad, since we need it more than ever these days. I was raised on gumption (sometimes called "spizzerinctum") and to this day I will use the word around the house . . . especially when trying to motivate the kids. I ran across it again while reading Robert Pirsig's *Zen and the Art of Motorcycle Maintenance* (now there's a great book title) as he was singing the praises of all that gumption represents. He writes:

> I like the word "gumption" because it's so homely and so forlorn and so out of style it looks as if it needs a friend and isn't likely to reject anyone who comes along. It's an old Scottish word, once used a lot by pioneers, but . . . seems to have all but dropped out of use. . . .
>
> A person filled with gumption doesn't sit around dissipating and stewing about things. He's at the front of the train of his own awareness, watching to see what's up the track and meeting it when it comes.[33]

A little later Pirsig applies it to life. Hiding his comments behind the word picture of repairing a motorcycle:

If you're going to repair a motorcycle, an adequate supply of gumption is the first and most important tool. If you haven't got that you might as well gather up all the other tools and put them away, because they won't do you any good.

Gumption is the psychic gasoline that keeps the whole thing going. If you haven't got it, there's no way the motorcycle can possibly be fixed. But if you have got it and know how to keep it, there's absolutely no way in the whole world that motorcycle can keep from getting fixed. It's bound to happen. Therefore the thing that must be monitored at all times and preserved before anything else is gumption.[34]

Seems a shame the old word has dropped through the cracks, especially since quitting is now more popular than finishing. I agree with that author, who'd like to start a whole new academic field on the subject. Can't you just see this entry in some college catalog: "Gumptionology 101." That'll never be, however, since gumption is better caught than taught. As is true of most other character traits, it is woven so subtly into the fabric of one's life that few ever stop and identify it. It is hidden like thick steel bars in concrete columns supporting ten-lane freeways. Gumption may be hidden, but it's an important tool for getting a job done.

Gumption enables us to save money rather than spend every dime we make. It keeps us at a hard task, like building a tedious model or completing an add-on or practicing piano or losing weight—and keeping it lost . . . or reading the Bible all the way through in a year's time. Most folks get a little gumption in their initial birth packet, but it's a tool that rusts rather quickly. Here's some sandpaper.

1. *Gumption begins with a firm commitment.* Daniel "made up his mind" (1:8) long before he was dumped in a Babylonian boot camp. Joshua didn't hesitate to declare his commitment in his famous "as for me and my house" speech (24:15) before the Israelis. Isaiah says he "set his face like flint" (50:7), which is another way of saying he firmly decided. Instead of starting with a bang, it's the human tendency to ponder, to rethink, to fiddle around with an idea until it's awash in a slimy swamp of indefiniteness. An old recipe for a rabbit dish starts out, "First, catch the rabbit." That puts first things first. No rabbit, no dish. You want gumption to continue to the end? Start strong!

2. *Gumption means being disciplined one day at a time.* Rather than focusing on the whole enchilada, take it in bite-size chunks. The whole of any objective can overwhelm even the most courageous. Writing a book? Do so one page at a time. Running a marathon? Those 26 plus miles are run one step at a time. Trying to master a new language? Try one word at a time. There are 365 days in the average year. Divide any project by 365 and none seem all that intimidating, do they? It will take daily discipline (*a la* Proverbs 19:27), not annual discipline.

3. *Gumption includes being alert to subtle temptations.*
Robert Pirsig referred to our being at the front of
the train of our own awareness, looking up the
track and being ready to meet whatever comes.
Gumption plans ahead . . . watching out for associ-
ations that weaken us (Proverbs 13:20), procrastina-
tion that steals from us (Proverbs 24:30-34), and
rationalizations that lie to us (Proverbs 13:4, 25:28).
People who achieve their goals stay alert. Our adver-
sary is a master strategist, forever fogging up our
minds with smokescreens, which "thicken" our
senses. If it were possible for God to die and He
died this morning, some wouldn't know it for three
or four days. Gumption stabs us awake, keeps us
wide-eyed and ready.

4. *Gumption requires the encouragement of accountability.*
People—especially close friends—keep our tanks
pumped full of enthusiasm. They communicate
"You can do it, you can make it" a dozen different
ways. At David's low-water mark, Jonathan stepped
in. Right when Elijah was ready to cash in everything, along came Elisha. With Paul was Timothy
. . . or Silas or Barnabas or Dr. Luke. People need
people, which is why Solomon came on so strong
about iron sharpening iron (Proverbs 27:17).

5. *Gumption comes easier when we remember that finishing
has its own unique rewards.* Jesus told the Father He
"accomplished" His assignment (John 17:4). On
more than one occasion Paul referred to "finishing
the course" (Acts 20:24, 2 Timothy 4:7). Those who

only start projects never know the surge of satisfaction that comes with slapping hands together, wiping away those beads of perspiration, and saying that beautiful four-letter word, "Done!" Desire accomplished is sweet to the soul.

Do you desire to have the character of Christ formed in you? No quest is more important. Are you underway? Good for you! If the journey seems extra long today, enjoy a gust of wind at your back from these words out of *The Living Bible*. It's one of those spizzerinctum Scriptures.

> *. . . let us not get tired of doing what is right, for after a while we will reap a harvest of blessing if we don't get discouraged and quit* (Galatians 6:9).

Today is unique! It has never occurred before and it will never be repeated. At midnight it will end, quietly, suddenly, totally. Forever. But the hours between now and then are opportunities with eternal possibilities. You will never again worship your Lord or share His love with someone *today*. With His enablement, live this day to the full—as if it were your last day on earth. It may be.

Read Galatians 6:1-10.

deep-water faith

A funny thing happened in Darlington, Maryland, several years ago. Edith, a mother of eight, was coming home from a neighbor's house one Saturday afternoon. Things seemed too quiet as she walked across her front yard. Curious, she peered through the screen door and saw five of her youngest children huddled together, concentrating on something. As she crept closer to them, trying to discover the center of attention, she could not believe her eyes. Smack dab in the middle of the circle were five baby skunks.

Edith screamed at the top of her voice, "Quick, children . . . run!" Each kid grabbed a skunk and ran.

Some days are like that, aren't they? You think you have plenty of problems as it is—and then you try to deal with them. When you do, they multiply.

Jesus was not preserved from such pressure when He was among us. On one particular occasion, things happened at such a rapid rate He could scarcely get His breath. I'm thinking of those events recorded in Luke 4:31-44. He was teaching on a regular basis in the synagogue. He was answering people's questions, facing their criticisms, dodging the Pharisees' and

Sadducees' bullets, casting out demons, living with all the complications that accompany increased popularity, healing the sick, confronting the forces of evil . . . it's all there. Check for yourself.

He attempted to find a quiet place, only to be found by "multitudes . . . searching for Him" who "tried to keep Him from going away from them" (Luke 4:42). No escape possible. The draining public kept right on siphoning His energy.

Ultimately, according to the fifth chapter of Luke, he found a place to be alone, at least somewhat alone. He stepped into a boat and took a seat. Once He caught His breath He "began teaching the multitudes from the boat." What a man! Though His emotions were spent and His body was weary, He stayed at it. At last, He was able to draw things to a close—at least with the crowd of people. But there was a bit of unfinished business Jesus needed to take care of. Let's let Luke describe it.

> And when He had finished speaking, He said to Simon, "Put out into the deep water and let down your nets for a catch."
>
> And Simon answered and said, "Master, we worked hard all night and caught nothing, but at Your bidding I will let down the nets" (5:4-5).

No one can criticize Peter for being reluctant. Old Simon knew those waters. Furthermore, he'd been at it all night and caught zilch. Hard work, no catch.

Naturally, the guy would frown and resist. But he wisely surrendered. What happened is nothing short of miraculous.

> *And when they had done this, they enclosed a great quantity of fish; and their nets began to break; and they signaled to their partners in the other boat, for them to come and help them. And they came, and filled both of the boats, so that they began to sink* (5:6-7).

Since I love to fish, I find that scene terribly inviting. I mean, so many fish both boats began to sink! My first thought? "What a way to go!" If you're gonna die, can anything be more satisfying to a fisherman than dying waist deep in fish?

I have caught forty big speckled trout off Matagorda Island in less than forty-five minutes. I've caught over thirty prize-winning salmon in Alaska in a little over an hour. I've caught my limit of walleye and northern pike early one morning in central Canada, an enormous ugly hammerhead shark off Miami, a yellow-fin tuna off the north shore of Kauai . . . but never have I ever been in a boat so heavy with fish that the thing began to sink!

That's because I have never fished with Jesus. When the Master of earth, sea, and skies calls the shots, things happen . . . which explains Peter's explosive reaction:

*But when Simon Peter saw that, he fell down at Jesus' feet,
saying, "Depart from me, for I am a sinful man, O Lord!"
For amazement had seized him and all his companions because
of the catch of fish which they had taken; and so also James
and John, sons of Zebedee, who were partners with Simon
. . . (vv. 8-10).*

Notice anything unusual? Earlier Peter called
Jesus "Master." After the miracle, "Lord." Gripped
with the realization that he was in the boat with the
living God, Peter sounds like Isaiah of old, "Woe is
me!" I find Jesus' words a little surprising.

*. . . And Jesus said to Simon, "Do not fear, from now on you
will be catching men" (v. 10).*

There the two of them stood, hip deep in fish,
and Jesus talks about "catching fish"? No. Fish meant
little to Him, merely an opportunity to teach a deeper
message by analogy. On His heart was "catching"
human beings. His real message was deep-water faith.
Did the fishermen get the message?

*And when they had brought their boats to land, they left
everything and followed Him (v. 11).*

Amazing, huh? Once they heard His invitation,
they literally dropped everything and ran.

Ponder "everything."

Their lifelong occupation. Their familiar surroundings. Their own goals. Their nets, boats, and

business. Everything. To be candid with you, I am impressed with their response. I've been thinking a lot about why.

I'm ready to suggest six reasons people are willing to drop everything and follow Jesus Christ. Each reason could be stated in a principle.

1. *Jesus chooses not to minister to others all alone.* He could, you realize. But He deliberately chooses not to. He could have rowed that boat Himself. He didn't (v. 3). He could've dropped those nets over the side. He didn't (v. 4). He certainly could've pulled up the nets choked with fish. Instead, they did (vv. 6-7). And did you notice? He specifically stated, "From now on you will be catching men" (v. 10).

2. *Jesus uses the familiar to do the incredible.* He came to their turf (lake, boat). He got into their place of work (fishing) and had them use their skills (nets). In such a familiar setting, He made them aware of incredible possibilities.

3. *Jesus moves us from the safety of the seen to the risks of the unseen.* Nothing significant occurred in shallow water. He specifically led them "out into the deep water" where nobody could touch bottom. It was not until they got out there that He commanded them to "Let down your nets." The deep is always full of uncertainties.

4. *Jesus proves the potential by breaking our nets and by filling our boats.* Not one of those salty, weary fisher-

men would've bet one denarius that there were so many fish in that lake. Certainly not where they just fished! When God's hand is on a situation, nets break, eyes bulge, deck planks groan, and boats almost sink. It's His way of putting the potential on display.

5. *Jesus conceals His surprises until we follow His leading.* Everything was business as usual on the surface. Boats didn't have a halo, nets didn't tingle at their touch, the lake water didn't glow. No. The divinely arranged surprise came only after they dropped the nets. Remember, it wasn't until he followed Jesus' instructions that Peter changed "Master" to "Lord."

6. *Jesus reveals His objective to those who release their security.* He could read their willingness in their faces. Then (and only then) did He tell them they'd be engaged in "catching men" (v. 10). And guess what—they jumped at the chance!

Is your life full of appointments, activities, hassles, and hurry? Are you finding all your security in your work . . . in your own achievements? Have you put the quest for character on temporary hold while you run faster and jockey for the pole position? Maybe it's time for a mental boat trip out into the deep. Take time to listen, lest you intensify your problem. And when Jesus says "Follow Me," do it. Unlike Edith's kids, drop everything and run.

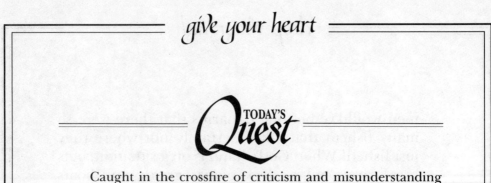

TODAY'S
Quest

Caught in the crossfire of criticism and misunderstanding on one side and people demands on the other, Jesus, "while it was still dark . . . arose and went out and departed to a lonely place . . ." and there He knelt in prayer (Mark 1:35). Feeling crushed by the crowd these days? Pushed into a corner from which there seems no escape? Anxiety reaching a fever pitch? Stop. Pray. Try turning it over to One who can handle your load.

Read Luke 5.

breaking free

A Whack on the Side of the Head is a book on how to break the inertia and unlock your mind for innovative thinking. While reading it I realized anew how easy it is to live out one's days with a locked-up mind. As a result, creativity is squelched and objectivity is squashed. The real tragedy is boredom. We become robot-like, thinking the expected, doing the predictable, missing the joy of fresh discovery. By adopting a creative outlook, as author Roger von Oech points out, we open ourselves to new possibilities and change. But that requires thinking outside the prison of common boundaries.

Johann Gutenberg is a superb example. What did he do? He simply combined two previously unconnected ideas to create an innovation. He refused to limit his thinking to the singular purpose of the wine press or to the solitary use of the coin punch. One day he entertained an idea no one else had ever thought of: "What if I took a bunch of coin punches and put them under the force of the wine press so that they left their images on paper instead of metal?" From that womb the printing press was born.

Let's face it, most of us have certain attitudes which seize our thoughts and lock them up in Status Quo Penitentiary. Frowning guards named Fear, Perfectionism, Laziness, and Traditionalism keep a constant vigil lest we attempt to escape. I am indebted to von Oech for this list of ten "mental locks" that keep us prisoners:

1. "THE RIGHT ANSWER."
2. "THAT'S NOT LOGICAL."
3. "FOLLOW THE RULES."
4. "BE PRACTICAL."
5. "AVOID AMBIGUITY."
6. "TO ERR IS WRONG."
7. "PLAY IS FRIVOLOUS."
8. "THAT'S NOT MY AREA."
9. "DON'T BE FOOLISH."
10. "I'M NOT CREATIVE."[35]

Each "mental lock" is hazardous to innovative thinking. Because we have heard them (and said them) so often, they are cast in concrete. Nothing short of "a whack on the side of the head" can dislodge the assumptions that keep us thinking "same song, fourth verse."

What is true mentally is also true spiritually. Our thoughts and expectations can become so determined by the predictable, we no longer see beyond the walls. In fact, we not only resist innovations, we resent anyone who suggests them. Example? The Pharisees. They were forever on Jesus' case because His message and style—really, the freedom with which He went about His life—constantly challenged their steel-trap mindset. What they considered truth He considered tradition. What they said was obedience He said was hypocrisy. Whom they called leader and teacher ("Rabbi") He called "blind guides." He even had the audacity to say, "You invalidate the Word of God for the sake of your tradition," which caused the disciples later on to give this wide-eyed report, "Do you know that the Pharisees were offended . . . ?" That always makes me smile. We're talking major "whack on the side of the head"! Breaking free, however, requires it.

Before we get to feeling too smug, let's be honest enough to admit there's a little Pharisee in all of us. Harmful though it is, we find a lot of security in our iron bars and solid walls. You and I could list at least ten "spiritual locks" that hold us prisoner. Each one comes naturally, is fed by pride, and permeates the ranks of Christianity. Tragically, this ball-and-chain mentality keeps us from giving ourselves in fresh, innovative ways to others. One such spiritual lock would certainly be *"I cannot forgive."* To beef up our determination we rehearse the wrongs done against us, buttressing the gate named Revenge. A Tolstoy story comes to mind:

> An honest and hardworking Russian peasant named Aksenov left his dear wife and family for a few days to visit a nearby fair. He spent his first overnight at an inn during which a murder was committed. The

murderer placed the murder weapon in the sleeping peasant's bag. The police discovered him that way in the morning. He was stuck in prison for twenty-six years, surviving on bitter hopes of revenge. One day the real murderer was imprisoned with him and soon charged with an escape attempt. He had been digging a tunnel that Aksenov alone had witnessed. The authorities interrogated the peasant about his crime granting him at long last his opportunity for revenge, for on the peasant's word his enemy would be flogged almost to death.

Aksenov was asked to bear witness to the crime, but instead of jumping at the chance, the grace of God suddenly wells up in the peasant's heart, and he finds the darkness in him has fled, and he is filled with light. He finds himself saying to the officers: "I saw nothing."

That night the guilty criminal makes his way to the peasant's bunk and, sobbing on his knees, begs his forgiveness. And again the light of Christ floods the peasant's heart. "God will forgive you," said he. "Maybe I am a hundred times worse than you." And at these words his heart grew light and the longing for home left him.[36]

You say you want to be different? You want to risk being innovative? You really desire to break free from your pharisaical ways but don't know where to begin? Start here. I don't know of anything more consuming, more constraining, than refusing to forgive. People who truly give their hearts are those who readily forgive their offenders. Go ahead and do the hard thing.

If it's a "whack on the side of the head" you need to get off the dime, consider yourself whacked. There's no better place to begin than with forgiveness. This single truth will break the inertia and unlock your prison, freeing you to fulfill your quest for character.

He is Lord! We see it often. We sing it often. But do we realize its significance? Has it become an idle cliché rather than a declaration of commitment . . . the ultimate risk? Only you can answer for yourself. *Lord* means "one having full authority, ruler, to whom service and obedience are due." Stop and think. Ask, "*Is* He Lord?" before you sing "He *is* Lord!"

Read Matthew 18:21-35.

conclusion

For over two hundred pages I have been emphasizing the quest for character. Some of the qualities God forms in our hearts are to be guarded, carefully and consistently kept. But other qualities are to be given, freely and fully released. Our hearts aren't always to be protected from intrusion. Sometimes we are to let ourselves go . . . allow ourselves to be broken . . . give ourselves away. It takes both guarding and giving. As Aristotle once wrote:

> To enjoy the things we ought and to hate the things we ought has the greatest bearing on excellence of character.

Like a coin, unless we display two distinctly different sides, we will lack authenticity and value. Throughout our days—year after year—the lifelong process of character development goes on. While we wait, God works. So let's not grow weary. The more He hammers and files, shapes and chisels, the more we are being conformed to the image of His Son. Be patient. Trust Him even in the pain, even though the process is long. God honors those who wait on Him.

But let's not *just* wait! These days of development are more than a passive process where we sit grim-faced as if hiding in an attic, praying for grace as the quest for character transpires.

I think we need a change of emphasis. I'm not suggesting we dump all that fine scoop about waiting and trusting. What I am suggesting is that we realize the possibility of running it into the ground. We can get so good at waiting we never act . . . cobwebs form, a layer of dust settles, we yawn and passively mutter, "Maybe, someday . . . " as we let opportunities slip away. Some people are more wait-conscious than a roomful of heavies in an aerobics class. They have this crazy idea that until we're everything we should be, we need to put most of life on hold. Everything, they feel, should wait until the quest is complete. I mean everything! Like having friends over for ice cream. Like going on a picnic. Like using the crystal and fine china. Like celebrating a birthday . . . or slipping away for a weekend of relaxation and romance . . . or splurging and taking a cruise or traveling abroad . . . or sailing for a day . . . or planning ahead and spending a week away with all the family. "Naw, not now, not this year; but *maybe, someday.* . . ."

Don't wait! The quest for character is an important process, for sure. But to back off from everything until all things are nailed down nice and tidy could result in something you regret for the rest of your days. I realized this anew when I read an article that appeared in the *Los Angeles Times.* If it doesn't get you off the dime, nothing will. A lady named Ann Wells writes:

> My brother-in-law opened the bottom drawer of my sister's bureau and lifted out a tissue-wrapped package.

"This," he said, "is not a slip. This is lingerie." He discarded the tissue and handed me the slip. It was exquisite: silk, handmade and trimmed with a cobweb of lace. The price tag with an astronomical figure on it was still attached.

"Jan bought this the first time we went to New York, at least eight or nine years ago. She never wore it. She was saving it for a special occasion. Well, I guess this is the occasion."

He took the slip from me and put it on the bed with the other clothes we were taking to the mortician. His hands lingered on the soft material for a moment, then he slammed the drawer shut and turned to me.

"Don't ever save anything for a special occasion. Every day you're alive is a special occasion."

I remembered those words through the funeral and the days that followed when I helped him and my niece attend to all the sad chores that follow an unexpected death. I thought about them on the plane returning to California from the midwestern town where my sister's family lives. I thought about all the things that she hadn't seen or heard or done. I thought about the things that she had done without realizing that they were special.

I'm still thinking about his words, and they've changed my life. . . .

I'm not "saving" anything; we use our good china and crystal for every special event—such as losing a pound, getting the sink unstopped, the first camellia blossom. . . .

"Someday" and "one of these days" are losing their grip on my vocabulary. If it's worth seeing or hearing or doing, I want to see and hear and do it now.

I'm trying very hard not to put off, hold back, or save anything that would add laughter and luster to our lives.

And every morning when I open my eyes I tell myself that it is special.[37]

My friend, life may be a jungle of difficulties and disappointments. Times may be hard and people may be demanding, but never forget that life is *special*. All of life. The pleasurable days as well as the painful ones. The Wednesdays as well as the weekends. The holidays as well as the days after. Days that seem insignificant and boring just as much as those when we get to see the President or receive a promotion or win a marathon. Every single day is a special day. God is at work in you!

So? So drink every moment to the full. Don't let the quest for character rob your joy or make you anxious. Stay sweet. Be positive. Stand tall. Face each dawn with fresh resolve. You're being conformed to the image of Christ. It's happening! He who began the quest will finish it.

Trust me, if Ballard could find the *Titanic* in a mere thirteen years, God can accomplish His goal in your lifetime. Rather than deciding to grit your teeth and bear it, why not live it up and enjoy it?

With God at work, you are in for the time of your life.

SET THEM AN EXAMPLE
BY DOING WHAT IS GOOD . . .
—*TITUS 2:7*

Also available by Charles R. Swindoll:

Books:
    Come Before Winter
    Compassion: Showing Care in a Careless World
    Dropping Your Guard
    Encourage Me
    For Those Who Hurt
    Growing Deep in the Christian Life
    Growing Strong in the Seasons of Life
    Hand Me Another Brick
    Improving Your Serve
    Killing Giants, Pulling Thorns
    Leadership: Influence that Inspires
    Living Above the Level of Mediocrity
    Living on the Ragged Edge
    Recovery: When Healing Takes Time
    Standing Out
    Starting Over
    Strengthening Your Grip
    Strike the Original Match
    Three Steps Forward, Two Steps Back
    Victory: A Winning Game Plan for Life
    You and Your Child

Booklets:

Anger	*Leisure*
Attitudes	*The Lonely Whine of the Top Dog*
Commitment	*Moral Purity*
Dealing with Defiance	*Our Mediator*
Demonism	*Peace in Spite of Panic*
Destiny	*Prayer*
Divorce	*Sensuality*
Eternal Security	*Singleness*
God's Will	*Stress*
Hope	*Tongues*
Impossibilities	*When Your Comfort Zone Gets the Squeeze*
Integrity	*Woman*

Films:
    People of Refuge
    Strengthening Your Grip

notes

1. Robert D. Ballard, "A Long Last Look at Titanic," *National Geographic* 170 (December 1986): 698-705.

2. Ibid.

3. "Terror on Side of a Steep Slope—Eyeball-to-Eyeball with a Rattler" *Los Angeles Times*, 4 November 1984, Sec. III, p. 1.

4. O. A. Battisti in *Quote Unquote*, ed. Lloyd Cory (Wheaton, Ill.: Victor Books, 1977), p. 112.

5. Poem by Ralph Waldo Emerson quoted in *Freedom for Ministry* by Richard John Neuhaus (San Francisco: Harper & Row, 1956), p. 90.

6. From an unpublished speech by Dr. Joseph Bayly entitled "Guarding Our Hearts." Presented at West Suburban Ministerial Fellowship in Wheaton, Illinois, in April 1986. Used by permission.

7. M. Scott Peck, *People of the Lie* (New York: Simon & Schuster, 1983), p. 221.

8. See Frank Sartwell, "The Small Satanic Worlds of John Calhoun," *Smithsonian Magazine*, April 1970, p.68ff; and John B. Calhoun, "The Lemmings' Periodic Journeys Are Not Unique," *Smithsonian Magazine*, January 1971, p. 11. Used by permission.

9. David A Seamands, *Healing for Damaged Emotions* (Wheaton, Ill.: Victor Books, 1981), p. 95.

10. Joseph Bayly, "Psalm of Single-mindedness," *Psalms of My Life* (Wheaton, Ill.: Tyndale House, 1969), pp. 40-41. Used by permission.

11. V. Raymond Edman, *The Disciplines of Life* (Wheaton, Ill.: Scripture Press, 1948), p. 83.

12. Used by permission of the author.

13. Sabine Baring-Gould, "Onward Christian Soldiers."

14. Rippon's "Selection of Hymns" (1787), "How Firm a Foundation."

15. Ted Engstrom, *The Pursuit of Excellence* (Grand Rapids, Mich.: Zondervan Publishing House, 1982), pp. 81-82.

16. John Steinbeck, in a letter to Adlai Stevenson quoted by Billy Graham in *World Aflame* (New York: Doubleday & Co., 1965), p. 25.

17. Carle C. Zimmerman, *Family and Civilization* (New York: Harper & Brothers, 1947), pp. 776, 777.

18. Eugene Peterson, *Traveling Light* (Downer's Grove, Ill.: InterVarsity Press, 1982), p.67.

19. C.S. Lewis, *The Four Loves* (New York: Harcourt Brace Jovanovich, 1960), p. 169. Used by permission.

20. Sir Winston Churchill, "A Colossal Military Disaster," a speech to the House of Commons, June 4, 1940, *Great War Speeches* (London: Corgi Books, a division of Transworld Publishers Ltd., 1957), p. 22.

21. Peter Marshall, *The Prayers of Peter Marshall* edited and prefaced by Catherine Marshall (New York: Carmel New York Guidepost Associates, Inc., 1949), p. 33.

22. *Los Angeles Times*, 26 September 1985.

23. Reinhold Niebuhr, "Well-Intentioned Dragons" *Christianity Today*, 1985, p. 63.

24. Ken Medema, "If This Is Not a Place," © 1977. Published by Word Music. Used by permission.

25. Jaroslav Pelikan, *The Vindication of Tradition*, (New Haven, Conn.: Yale University Press, 1984), p. 65.

26. Reprinted with permission of Macmillan Publishing Company, "Wisdom" from *Collected Poems* by Sara Teasdale. Copyright 1917 by Macmillan Publishing Company, renewed 1945 by Mamie T. Wheless.

27. William Manchester, *American Caesar: Douglas MacArthur, 1880-1964* (Little, Brown and Company, 1978).

28. Robert E. Coleman, *The Master Plan of Evangelism* (Old Tappan, N.J.: Fleming H. Revell, 1963), p. 23.

29. Tom J. Fatjo, Jr., and Keith Miller, *With No Fear of Failure* (Waco, Tex.: Word Books, 1981), p. 23.

30. Anthony Campolo, *Who Switched the Price Tags?* (Waco, Tex.: Word Books, 1986), pp. 69-72. Used by permission.

31. Sir Winston Churchill, *Familiar Quotations* ed. John Bartlett (Boston, Mass.: Little, Brown and Company, 1980), p. 868.

32. Aleksandr Solzhenitsyn, *East and West* (New York: Harper & Row, 1980), p. 45.

33. Robert M. Pirsig, *Zen and the Art of Motorcycle Maintenance* (New York: Bantam Books, 1974), pp. 272, 273.

34. Ibid.

35. Roger von Oech, *A Whack on the Side of the Head* (New York: Warner Books, 1983), p. 9.

36. A paraphrase of a Tolstoy story from *Russian Stories and Legends* (Pantheon Books), as told by David A. Redding, *Amazed by Grace* (Old Tappan, N.J.: Fleming H. Revell, 1986), pp. 33-34.

37. "What Are We Waiting For?" *Los Angeles Times*, 14 April 1985. Used by permission.

scripture index

subject index